Caryl Phillips was born in St.Kitts and brought up in England. He has written extensively for stage, radio, television and the screen. His first play, *Strange Fruit*, premiered at the Sheffield Crucible Theatre in 1980, with subsequent productions in London and at the Liverpool Playhouse. *Where There is Darkness* and *The Shelter* both premiered at the Lyric Theatre, Hammersmith. In 2007 his adaptation of Simon Schama's *Rough Crossings* for the stage toured Britain. He has collaborated with Peter Hall, writing and co-producing a three-hour film of his first novel, *The Final Passage*, for Channel Four, for whom he also wrote the film *Playing Away*. In 2001 he adapted V. S. Naipaul's *The Mystic Masseur* for Merchant Ivory Films. He is the author of numerous books of non-fiction and fiction. *Dancing in the Dark* won the 2006 PEN Open Book Award, and *A Distant Shore* was long-listed for the Booker Prize and won the 2004 Commonwealth Writers' Prize. His other awards include the Martin Luther King Memorial Prize for *The European Tribe*, a Lannan Literary Award, a Guggenheim Fellowship, and the James Tait Black Memorial Prize for *Crossing the River*, which was also short-listed for the Booker Prize. He is a contributor to newspapers and magazines on both sides of the Atlantic, a Fellow of the Royal Society of Literature, and holds honorary doctorates from a number of universities. His most recent novel, *A View of the Empire at Sunset*, was published in 2018.

Caryl Phillips

PLAYS ONE

Strange Fruit

Where There is Darkness

The Shelter

OBERON BOOKS
LONDON

WWW.OBERONBOOKS.COM

First published in this collection in 2019 by Oberon Books Ltd
521 Caledonian Road, London N7 9RH
Tel: +44 (0) 20 7607 3637 / Fax: +44 (0) 20 7607 3629
e-mail: info@oberonbooks.com
www.oberonbooks.com

PB ISBN: 9781786827906
E ISBN: 9781786827913

Cover image: Haywood Magee/Getty Images

Printed and bound by 4EDGE Limited, Hockley, Essex, UK.
eBook conversion by Lapiz Digital Services, India.

Visit www.oberonbooks.com to read more about all our books and to buy them. You will
also find features, author interviews and news of any author events, and you can sign up
for e-newsletters and be the first to hear about our new releases.

Printed on FSC® accredited paper

10 9 8 7 6 5 4 3 2 1

Contents

STRANGE FRUIT

For Catherine

Characters

(In order of appearance)

MOTHER
VERNICE
SHELLEY
ERROL
ALVIN

A note on the language

The language in *Strange Fruit* has to be a careful mixture of West Indian English (patois), Standard English, and English working-class regional dialect. In the language one should be able to detect the socio-cultural confusion which undermines any immediate hopes of harmony within the body politic of the family.

Act One

SCENE ONE

The action takes place in the front room of the Marshalls' terraced house in one of England's inner city areas. Whilst the district is not a ghetto, it is hardly suburbia. The room is cramped but comfortable and tidy. In the D.R. wall is a door which leads to the hall, and subsequently to the front door. In the back wall (slightly right of centre) is another door, which can be concealed by the drawing of a curtain. This door leads upstairs to the bedrooms and the bathroom. In the D.L. wall is a door which leads to the kitchen. It is one of those that slides open, rather than pulls or pushes open. The main items of furniture are as follows: against the back wall there is a heavy sideboard, on top of which sits a brightly crocheted coverlet, a large plastic punchbowl and ladle, a yellow glass vase containing plastic flowers, and a box of paper tissues. D.R. is a cabinet full of crockery that has never been, and never will be used. In the centre of the display is a plate commemorating the Queen's Silver Jubilee. The cabinet also contains a few bottles of spirits, and on top of it sit the family photographs. D.L. is a small table underneath which there are some albums. A small stereo sits on top with the speakers placed on the floor either side, thus completing this nest of music. In the centre of the room is an imitation black leather settee with orange yellow cushions. U.L. slightly is the armchair to match. The room is completed by the television, which is D.L. by the stereo. As to the surroundings: the wallpaper is tasteless, and on the wall hang the usual trinkets. Sub-Athena prints, a circular mirror with a gnarled plastic, imitation brass border, and those birds made of pottery which are so arranged as to make it appear that they are migrating for the winter as they fly away, one after the other. The windows on the world are in the fourth wall. Acknowledgement of their presence is not necessary. As I said, the room is cramped, even claustrophobic, but tidy.

Lights up. 5 p.m. We hear a key in the front door and then the door slam. Enter MOTHER carrying a shopping bag. She shuts the door behind her, leans against it and sighs deeply. She looks like she has never had

13

a day's rest in her life but is still neat and immaculately turned out. She is in her late forties and both thinks and acts thoroughly, albeit with a somewhat premature autumnal serenity. Still through a small chink in her armour one can sense despair. She knows that most of what is going to happen is inevitable so she prepares for the worst, as ever. Clearly the twin concepts of love and fear are at the heart of her character. She puts down the bag, takes off her coat and drapes it over the back of the armchair. She moves across to the settee and sits alone with her thoughts for a moment.

VERNICE: *(From the kitchen.)* Girl, you back home yet? Vivien you hear me?

(She shuts the back door and comes through the open sliding door into the front room. VERNICE is portly, about the same age as MOTHER, and wears a brightly coloured headscarf, Scholl sandals, no tights, which, together with her happy-go-lucky demeanour, suggests an easy attitude to life, one which she likes to project. She enjoys unsettling people, but not in a vindictive manner. Humorously 'loud' at times, she enjoys her telly. For her, England's not so much the enemy. Life has always been a struggle for survival. England is just the place where things have crumbled, where she has seen her life move from a very healthy top gear to a very insecure first. She sees MOTHER and sucks her teeth.)

Girl, why yuh no answer me, nuh?

MOTHER: I was about to. You didn't give me time.

VERNICE: Girl, me give you plenty time. You ain't hear me calling you or something, nuh.

MOTHER: I was about to, but I've only just got home from school.

VERNICE: You too wicked, you know.

MOTHER: I thought I locked that back door before I left this morning.

14

VERNICE: Errol open it for me before he go out.

MOTHER: To go where?

VERNICE: Me ain't ask. He come a big man now, or you ain't notice. *(Sucks her teeth. Pause.)* Alvin coming back tonight? Me see all him things them on the line.

MOTHER: Where are they?

VERNICE: Girl, what you think it is me do with them, nuh? Me put them in the flickin' kitchen basket.

MOTHER: Tomorrow.

VERNICE: What you talking about tomorrow for, eh? Me put them in the damn basket today, girl.

MOTHER: Alvin is coming back tomorrow. I'm going to iron his clothes today.

VERNICE: Well, why you not say so instead of friggin' me up so.

MOTHER: *(Sighs.)* Would you like some tea, Vernice?

VERNICE: Uh hur. Come, lemme give you a hand, nuh. *(Makes no attempt to do so.)*

MOTHER: No, it's alright. *(She gets up and goes to the kitchen.)*

The electric kettle is still broken so I'm going to have to boil the water in a pan. It won't take long if that's alright with madam.

VERNICE: It's alright.

MOTHER: Is everything here?

VERNICE: *(Sucks her teeth.)* Girl, what you meaning now? Your arse beginning to sound off like twenty questions or something.

MOTHER: In the laundry basket?

VERNICE: What happen? You think me want to thief off some uh you son's clothes for me daughter to come dress up in them? *(Sucks her teeth.)*

MOTHER: Good God, Vernice, I just wondered if Errol had taken any away for I haven't had time to do his washing yet. I'm not accusing you of anything.

VERNICE: Well, me ain't know, girl. All me did was to bring in the basket and then me leave the boy to do his own thing, or whatever it is them all like to do.

MOTHER: I see.

VERNICE: Anyway, Alvin ain't the type of boy to mash up his own brother for thieving a pair uh socks. The pair of them getting on just fine in all the time me know them. Good spars.

MOTHER: Good what?

VERNICE: Good spars. Girl, you ain't up with the times, as usual.

(MOTHER comes through with two cups of tea – no saucers.)

MOTHER: Well, Alvin can get nasty at times about his things. He gets a bit overbearing.

VERNICE: Girl, you too bad sometimes. Why you don't leave the boys them alone, nuh? They still young and got plenty time for all that kinda thing. You should just be grateful that the pair uh them managing to keep themselves outa trouble with the police and thing.

MOTHER: Should be glad of what? Grateful for what! Vernice, my children have never been in any kind of trouble. My children are qualified, they have O-Levels and A-Levels and have both been to college, and you're telling me that I should be happy that they are managing to keep out of trouble.

16

VERNICE: *(Sucks her teeth.)* Girl, you know it mus' be hard for they with you all come a teacher and you always coming down so hard on they when they so young still. You too friggin' rough on they, you know.

MOTHER: I think I'm the best judge of that. Look Vernice, I've got work to do and I'm tired.

VERNICE: Me arse, I come round here to ask one favour of you but if you want me go…

MOTHER: Then for heaven's sake ask.

VERNICE: It's Charmain.

MOTHER: Well?

VERNICE: She ain't talking to me.

MOTHER: Again! Well, she must be saying something.

VERNICE: When Charmain decide she ain't talking, she ain't saying nothing to nobody, you hear me.

MOTHER: *(Sighs.)* How long's this been going on?

VERNICE: Only two or three days but Lord, with only me and she alone in the house it feel like weeks. Me think she must be missing having a father.

MOTHER: But, Vernice, it's eight years since Wilfred passed on.

VERNICE: You think I don't know that?

MOTHER: I'm sorry. What would you like me to do?

VERNICE: Girl, me ain't know, but I thought with you being a teacher and use to kids playing up and thing that mebbe you could talk to she and get some sense in she damn head.

MOTHER: Well, how's she doing at school?

VERNICE: Me ain't know girl. Last parents' evening she have is about two years ago now. She doing alright then.

MOTHER: Rubbish!

VERNICE: What you mean 'rubbish'? I tell you she doing alright then, or mebbe you think it just you all who is able to come intelligent, eh? Well don't come none of you hoity-toity ways with me girl, for me know you all long time and don't let you arse forget it, nuh.

MOTHER: Vernice, parents' evening is twice a year, and now she's in the fifth form you should be getting a fortnightly report.

VERNICE: And where you say me supposed to be getting all this from?

MOTHER: Well, hasn't she been giving you one?

VERNICE: *(Sucks her teeth.)* Giving me one what, girl? All she give me is one set uh filthy looks after the other. *(Pause.)* You think me oughta go and ask she for it?

MOTHER: Naturally. Look Vernice, you might have a better chance of finding out why she's acting like she's doing if you have a look at it.

VERNICE: I tell you me ain't even know she got the blasted thing. Look the hell, me going to have to ask she for it. *(Gets up.)* Lord, she ain't going to like this, for sure.

MOTHER: She's not supposed to like it. It's her duty for God's sake.

VERNICE: Me going ask she.

(VERNICE goes out via the kitchen. MOTHER rises and takes the two cups into the kitchen. She picks up her bag of shopping en route. She comes back through, after a few moments, with the basket full of

*ALVIN's, clothes and begins to sort through them. We hear the back
door slam. Re-enter VERNICE with the report.)*

MOTHER: Did you get it?

VERNICE: Me have it. The girl just throw it at me and storm
out the house.

MOTHER: Well open it then. Go ahead.

VERNICE: You open it.

(MOTHER reluctantly takes it, opens it, and begins to read.)

Well?

MOTHER: She's not doing too well.

VERNICE: What?

MOTHER: Well, you do know that they've moved her out
of the GCE into the CSE stream, which means that her
chances of ending up with an HND or even a BSc rather
than just an OND are greatly diminished.

VERNICE: Fockin' CSE, GCE, CND, this that and the other
is just one seta flickin' initial to me. What the hell the
matter with she?

MOTHER: Well, nothing that a...

VERNICE: Nothing? If me can't talk to me own daughter then
something is the matter.

MOTHER: I think you'd better go and see her teacher. She
says here that she's also worried about her absenteeism.

VERNICE: What fockin' absenteeism? The girl ain't had a day
off school since she eight.

MOTHER: But...

19

VERNICE: No fockin' but about it. I just about had she up to me back teeth. *(She stands.)*

MOTHER: Sit down, Vernice, and listen. I'll come round with you and we'll talk to her together if you like.

VERNICE: No point. She just gone off. Who the hell she think she is anyway playing absent from she school.

MOTHER: Okay, then, I'll call round tomorrow after work.

VERNICE: What you mean work tomorrow?

MOTHER: I mean what I said. Work tomorrow.

VERNICE: You mean you ain't coming out on strike with us then?

MOTHER: Vernice, what do you mean coming out on strike with 'us'. Since when have you done a day's work in your life.

VERNICE: Girl, me a widow with a house and daughter to look after. Don't forget me ain't have no man in me house either.

MOTHER: Hmmm.

VERNICE: What you say?

MOTHER: Nothing.

VERNICE: Come again.

MOTHER: I said nothing.

VERNICE: Lemme tell you girl. One day you going have to join the coloured race and you best watch you all step that nobody kick you in you arse when you decide it time you want to do so.

(Gets up.)

I going to see me affairs.

(She goes out via the kitchen. MOTHER sighs and begins to unwind again. After a few moments she hears the front doorbell.)

MOTHER: Damn!

(She wanted to be alone. She goes out to the hall and we hear her opening the front door.)

Hello Shelley. What brings you around at this time?

SHELLEY: Nothing really, Miss, except I've come to drop off these albums for Errol.

MOTHER: Well, come on in then. You don't have to wait on ceremony in this house, you know.

SHELLEY: Yeah, I know. Thanks.

(Enter MOTHER, followed by SHELLEY. She is sixteen, quietly pretty with dark brown shoulder-length hair, and she wears little make-up. She dresses with care, preferring a skirt or a dress to trousers. No jewellery or nail varnish: she doesn't need it.)

MOTHER: Well, how long has it been raining?

SHELLEY: Not long really. It only just started up again about ten minutes ago, but it's really coming down now.

MOTHER: Oh dear.

SHELLEY: But it looks like it's gonna stop, though. One of those quick blasts that you sometimes get.

MOTHER: Take off your coat and hang it up. I'll open out your umbrella in the kitchen if you like.

SHELLEY: Yeah, thanks.

(MOTHER takes the umbrella and goes off. SHELLEY raises her voice so that she can be heard.)

Anyhow Miss, it's bad enough being trapped in this place, the city I mean, without having it raining all the time.

MOTHER: *(Coming back through.)* What do you mean trapped? You're not trapped.

SHELLEY: I am Miss. Where am I gonna get the money from to catch a bus or even a train to the country or the seaside? Me mum and dad ain't half tight. They must think I can live on Biafran rations or something.

MOTHER: I see. Well, you could get a job I suppose.

SHELLEY: Yeah, but how am I gonna get some work done to pass my exams. I go out most nights as it is. If it isn't one thing it's another. *(Pause.)* And besides, I don't think Errol would like it. He's always on about a woman's place and the man being the 'hunter'.

MOTHER: The what?

SHELLEY: The 'hunter'.

MOTHER: You don't want to take any notice of that rubbish.

SHELLEY: No, I suppose not. *(Pause.)* He isn't at home is he, Miss?

MOTHER: What's the panic?

SHELLEY: Nothing.

(SHELLEY sighs. Pause.)

MOTHER: Are you feeling alright, Shelley?

SHELLEY: Course Miss, why?

(Pause. MOTHER looks closely at her.)

MOTHER: Look Shelley, is it Errol?

SHELLEY: Miss, it's just that sometimes it can get bad and he just cuts me off. God, I even have to lie sometimes about what I'm thinking in case he falls out with me.

MOTHER: What do you mean?

SHELLEY: Well, I'm going to have to, Miss. I can't help it unless I leave home for two days or something.

MOTHER: You're going to have to what?

SHELLEY: To buy and eat something British, break the strike. I'm going to have to get on a bus and what have you, 'cause I just have to. I've got to get to school and whatnot. but if I tell him that I'd done any of this then he'd kill me.

MOTHER: Don't be stupid, Shelley.

SHELLEY: Don't call me stupid, Miss. Everyone calls me stupid. Just because I'm not coloured doesn't mean I'm stupid or that I can't do anything.

MOTHER: Shelley.

SHELLEY: You don't know what it's like, Miss. To be gradually cut out of somebody's life after two years because they've suddenly decided that you're not right or something. He hardly talks to me, he hardly says anything without being right, and I hardly say anything without being wrong, and all the time it's us and them, or you and I, or our side and your side, and I can't stand it, Miss. I can't.

MOTHER: Calm down, Shelley. You came for a chat with me and I'm grateful. I'm listening.

SHELLEY: Yes Miss.

MOTHER: Listen, why don't you call it a day, then? You know, the pair of you split up. Tell him it's over.

SHELLEY: I can't.

MOTHER: Oh come off it Shelley, what do you mean you can't.

(SHELLEY begins to cry.)

Shelley, what's the matter?

SHELLEY: I'm sorry, Miss.

MOTHER: There's nothing to be sorry about, after all…

SHELLEY: Miss, I think I'm having a baby.

MOTHER: You only think you're having a baby?

SHELLEY: I'm pretty sure, Miss. I'm getting the results of my tests back tomorrow afternoon. *(Pause.)*

MOTHER: Have you told Errol?

SHELLEY: No Miss.

MOTHER: Why not?

SHELLEY: I told you, Miss. He doesn't seem to pay much attention to me these days

MOTHER: Well, he's obviously paid some attention to you.

SHELLEY: Miss…

(She begins to cry anew.)

MOTHER: I'm sorry, Shelley. What are we going to do?

SHELLEY: I don't know, Miss.

MOTHER: Well someone's going to have to tell him.

SHELLEY: Yes, Miss.

MOTHER: And you'd rather it wasn't you?

SHELLEY: It's not that, Miss. I just want to make sure first.

MOTHER: And your parents. Do they know?

SHELLEY: You're the only person I've told, Miss.

MOTHER: What about your friends?

SHELLEY: You're the only person I've told, Miss. *(Pause.)* Miss, it wasn't his fault.

MOTHER: What do you mean?

SHELLEY: I'm not on the pill, Miss.

MOTHER: Well, didn't you use some kind of protection?

SHELLEY: Miss – *(She begins to cry again.)*

MOTHER: Shelley.

SHELLEY: I told him I was on the pill, Miss.

MOTHER: You told him…Why?

SHELLEY: I had to, Miss, or he might not have wanted to keep going out with me. I can't go on the pill, Miss, because I'm Catholic and if me parents found out that I was on it they'd kill me.

MOTHER: I suppose that also rules out an abortion.

SHELLEY: I don't want to kill it, Miss. It's something to share. I can't kill it. Please Miss, I can't.

MOTHER: Alright, Shelley, I understand. It's going to be alright. I think we had both better have a drink. Brandy?

(SHELLEY nods. MOTHER gets up and crosses to the cabinet.)

It doesn't look as if there's much we can do until tomorrow then?

SHELLEY: No, Miss.

MOTHER: Are you going out tonight?

SHELLEY: I think so, Miss. Errol said he'd meet me at about eight o'clock by the club.

(MOTHER crosses and hands her the drink.)

MOTHER: Plenty of time, then. Shall I show you my album whilst we have a drink?

SHELLEY: Miss?

(MOTHER crosses and takes the album out of a bottom drawer in the sideboard.)

MOTHER: Photograph album. From home. *(Looks at watch.)* It's not even six yet so you won't be late.

SHELLEY: *(Wiping her eyes on the back of her hand.)* I know, Miss. *(Pause.)* Are there any pictures of Errol as a little boy?

MOTHER: *(Laughs.)* Plenty. *(She comes and sits down.)* Hasn't he shown you this before?

SHELLEY: No, Miss. I once sneaked out a load of pictures of me as a kid, but he just said that pictures negate progress and that was that.

MOTHER: Did you want anything in your brandy?

SHELLEY: I don't know, Miss. It's alright like this I think…

MOTHER: Fine.

(They settle down to look at the album. Almost immediately they hear the sound of a key in the door.)

SHELLEY: God, Miss, it's Errol. Tell him I only came round to drop off the records.

(She stands.)

I'd better be off now.

(MOTHER closes the album. Enter ERROL from the hall. He is carrying a large parcel in brown paper which he leans off against the back wall. ERROL is twenty-one and of medium height and build. He likes to think of himself as good-looking, but prefers not to dress in a sharp way for fear of being accused of vanity. So he dresses untidily, knowing that it's the mind that matters, but he will occasionally pin on a badge of protest only to remove it a few days later thinking that he's 'sold out'. He can't decide whether or not to grow an Afro, but nevertheless keeps his shapeless hair tidy-ish.)

ERROL: What are you doing here?

SHELLEY: It's okay. I'm just off.

ERROL: Oh great. Brilliant answer.

SHELLEY: I only came round to drop off some records. So?

MOTHER: What's the parcel?

ERROL: Oh that. It's a parcel.

(He moves and sits. Pause.)

MOTHER: Wipe your nose, Errol. How old are you now?

(Wiping his nose on his sleeves.)

ERROL: Forty-three, nearly forty-four.

(MOTHER tosses her head and gets up to put away the photograph album.)

SHELLEY: It's still alright about tonight then?

ERROL: What's that?

SHELLEY: Tonight?

ERROL: *(Gesturing with his hand.)* No, that.

MOTHER: Don't be stupid.

ERROL: Well I know what it is, but what's it doing out?

MOTHER: Shelley and I were just going to look at some pictures. *(She comes back and sits.)* I don't know why you don't take more interest.

ERROL: In what?

MOTHER: Things.

ERROL: *(Sucks his teeth.)* Pictures negate progress.

SHELLEY: I think pictures are nice.

ERROL: You would, wouldn't you?

MOTHER: Come on now, stop bickering.

ERROL: Who's bickering? We're not bickering, it's you.

MOTHER: Fine. Anyhow Shelley, if you ever want to have a look at them, you know where they are.

SHELLEY: Thanks.

ERROL: She's got her own 'roots'. What are you forcing her for?

SHELLEY: She's not forcing me.

MOTHER: No, I'm not. It's just natural to want to know something about your boyfriend's past.

ERROL: Well, I live in a world of reality.

MOTHER: Pardon?

ERROL: A world of reality and brutality.

SHELLEY: I'd best go now.

MOTHER: Look, for heaven's sake sit down, Shelley, and I'll get the pair of you some tea before you go out.

SHELLEY: I don't know if I should.

MOTHER: Oh come on, sit down. Nobody's going to bite you. I'll just see what we've got.

(She goes into the kitchen. SHELLEY sits down. Pause.)

ERROL: Me Momma goin' to cook up some goat for yer, you know that?

SHELLEY: Pardon?

MOTHER: *(Shouting through.)* Errol, stop that.

ERROL: She goin' cook up some good soulfood an' plenty yam.

MOTHER: *(Amused.)* Look Shelley, take no notice of him.

ERROL: Shelley, girl. I hopes yer knows we all eat cat food, you know. Kit-e-Kat, man, an' a big tinna Whiskas on a Sunday.

MOTHER: Errol, don't be stupid. Anyway, have you seen the price of cat food lately?

SHELLEY: What you on about? Come on, tell us.

MOTHER: *(Comes through from the kitchen.)* We're having salad, Shelley. Don't take any notice of him, he's just being silly.

ERROL: Salad! It's bloody freezing outside. It's only just stopped raining.

MOTHER: Well, I haven't got anything else to give you.

ERROL: I thought you said you were going to do some shopping today for Alvin coming back.

MOTHER: So?

ERROL: So, where is it?

MOTHER: It's in the kitchen. But I've only got one pair of hands you know.

ERROL: But it's turned six o'clock. It's not your hands you've been sat on for God knows how long.

MOTHER: Errol, no sooner had I set foot in the house than Vernice appeared...

ERROL: Oh God.

MOTHER: ...and after I'd got rid of her, Shelley came round, not that I minded Shelley coming round, but where am I supposed to get time to cook in? I'm not a magician.

(She goes back into the kitchen.)

SHELLEY: She's right, Errol. Vernice can't half talk, you know. Remember that time I first met her an...

ERROL: Since when have you been an expert on Vernice and post-teaching fatigue?

SHELLEY: Well, she's right, isn't she?

ERROL: You haven't answered the question. Well... *(He waits impatiently then sucks his teeth.)* Hey! She came round here before.

MOTHER: I'm not deaf, Errol.

ERROL: Well, you're in there. I thought you might not hear.

MOTHER: *(Coming through.)* Well I'm in here now and I can hear perfectly well, thank you. Before when?

ERROL: Well, she came round and brought the clothes in off the line. Her and her lover man, Stanley the flying milkman.

MOTHER: What! You mean he helped her?

ERROL: Yeah. A real two-pronged attack it was. Is something the matter with that? He ain't got bugs you know. Alvin's clothes are still fit for human consumption or whatever.

MOTHER: I'm aware of the fact that Stanley hasn't got bugs. He was probably just passing, that's all.

ERROL: Oh come off it. At one o'clock in the afternoon? What milkman do you know that comes round at one in the afternoon? To deliver milk, anyway. I can just hear it now. 'Yes dear, that's right. We've got the only black milkman in Britain, but the unfortunate thing is he can't get out of bed before noon, and he doesn't start his round till after one, poor thing. They have these parties, you know. It takes a toll on them. Such a shame!'

MOTHER: Rubbish! Stanley's always here by eight at the latest.

ERROL: Exactly. And he's always back round there by eleven.

MOTHER: Anyway, Errol. It's none of your business. French, blue cheese or mayonnaise dressing, Shelley?

ERROL: She don't know the difference.

MOTHER: Errol!

SHELLEY: Blue cheese, please Miss.

MOTHER: It'll be ready in a minute. We can eat it in here on our knees if you like.

SHELLEY: That's fine, honest. Great.

(MOTHER smiles and goes back in the kitchen.)

ERROL: What is?

SHELLEY: Eating it off our knees.

ERROL: Oh I see. You sound like someone's doing you a favour. *(To MOTHER again.)* Anyway, what did Vernice want?

MOTHER: She's worried about Charmain.

ERROL: She's cracked.

MOTHER: Who is?

ERROL: Charmain, though I suppose both of them might be.

MOTHER: That's not very nice.

ERROL: Neither is Vernice.

MOTHER: You went to middle school with Charmain, didn't you, Shelley?

SHELLEY: Yes, Miss. We were in the same set for nearly everything.

MOTHER: Do you still see her now?

SHELLEY: Well, only about. She's changed a bit.

ERROL: I told you she's cracked. Bloody loony.

MOTHER: Errol, grow up.

SHELLEY: She's sort of gone into herself a bit.

ERROL: Pervert as well.

(MOTHER comes in with three salads on a large tray. She gives ERROL an angry glare.)

MOTHER: It's not very much, Shelley, but I hope it's alright.

SHELLEY: Looks great, Miss. I've never had blue cheese before.

MOTHER: Well, you should have said and I could have given you something else.

SHELLEY: No, it's okay. I wanted to try it anyway.

MOTHER: Well just say if you don't like it.

ERROL: Hey, Shelley. You know it makes you want to…

MOTHER: Errol!

ERROL: Alright. Alright.

SHELLEY: It's nice.

MOTHER: Shall I put the television on whilst you eat?

ERROL: God, no.

MOTHER: But it's the news.

ERROL: Oh, and I suppose that makes it alright.? 'Today sixty-eight youths were sentenced for conspiring to stand on a street corner… All sixty-eight were black.' It's only when you look up that you realise it's a bleeding black newscaster talking. Bloody Uncle Tom.

MOTHER: For heaven's sake, Errol, it's not all like that.

ERROL: Oh yeah.

MOTHER: Well, do you want to listen to some records then? Shelley, perhaps you'd like to put on one of those you brought round for Errol, or perhaps I'll put one of mine on if you like.

SHELLEY: That'd be great, Miss.

ERROL: Oh God. Here we go. Johnny 'oh haven't I been out in the sun a long time' Mathis.

MOTHER: Well, he's not as bad as you.

ERROL: Huh.

(Silence. ERROL is stung.)

SHELLEY: *(To ERROL.)* Laurie Cunningham was on the telly yesterday. Did you see it?

(No answer.)

MOTHER: No I didn't. Was it good?

SHELLEY: Great.

MOTHER: Did you see it, Errol?

ERROL: No.

MOTHER: What's the matter? Have you given up supporting him?

ERROL: I never supported him. You don't support individuals. You support teams.

SHELLEY: Errol supports West Bromwich Albion.

MOTHER: But he doesn't play for them anymore, does he?

ERROL: So what?

SHELLEY: It's alright though for Cyrille Regis and Brendon Batson still do. They're his heroes now.

ERROL: Look, I don't have heroes, right! People who make heroes only have to go through the ritual of breaking them at some point and I can do without that kind of hassle.

MOTHER: What's got into you?

ERROL: Nothing.

MOTHER: Well something's the matter.

ERROL: Nothing's the matter, right? N-O-T-H-I-N-G. Nothing.

MOTHER: We're not stupid, Errol. We can spell.

ERROL: Huh!

MOTHER: And what's that supposed to mean?

ERROL: It's supposed to mean what it sounded like.

MOTHER: I'm not a child, you know. I'm not one of your college friends or your Black Front friends or whatever you call them. You can't go around treating me like dirt and don't you forget it, showing off like a five-year-old.

ERROL: Forget what? Forget what?

MOTHER: I'm in no mind to argue with you.

ERROL: No mind to what? Well?

SHELLEY: I think I'd best be off now and get changed for tonight.

MOTHER: Okay then, Shelley, Errol will see you out.

ERROL: Will he hell. She knows where the door is.

SHELLEY: I'm full up, Miss, but it was great. You don't mind if I leave this bit, do you? *(She stands up.)*

MOTHER: Of course not. Look, I'll just get your umbrella for you.

(MOTHER goes to the kitchen for the umbrella and comes back into the front room.)

SHELLEY: See you at eight, Errol.

(He nods. SHELLEY and MOTHER leave the room and we hear MOTHER let SHELLEY out of the front door. ERROL pokes at his food. MOTHER comes back in.)

MOTHER: I suppose you think that was clever.

ERROL: Think what was clever?

MOTHER: What you've just done.

ERROL: What have I just done?

MOTHER: You know damn well what you've just done. How long do you think you can keep pushing that girl around like that? She's not a toy or a game. She's got feelings

35

too. Well? How long do you think you can keep pushing people around, full stop.

ERROL: I'm not pushing anybody around, and if they think that I am, well, it's their lookout isn't it?

MOTHER: Errol, look at me.

ERROL: I am looking at you.

MOTHER: What's the matter?

ERROL: *(Slams down his plate.)* For Christ's sake, stop asking me that question! There's nothing the matter with me. I'm my own man and if you think that something's wrong with me then it's your lookout. You go ahead and burn yourself up with pointless worry. I'm fine. Doing just fine, thanks. I want to finish my tea in peace.

MOTHER: Doing fine. You must think I'm stupid. Where do you spend the day?

ERROL: None of your business.

MOTHER: I'll tell you where. In that stinking rathole they call a cafe.

ERROL: Who calls it a rathole?

MOTHER: Everyone calls it a rathole.

ERROL: I don't call it a rathole.

MOTHER: You're not everyone and the sooner you wake up to that fact the better. Just look at yourself in the mirror! Do you ever do that? Twenty-one, a second-class degree in Economics from a good college, the world in front of you, and you sit on your arse all day with those jigaboos and drug addicts talking about Africa.

ERROL: Talking about what?

MOTHER: I don't know what you all talk about, but why don't you go and get a job like everyone else?

ERROL: Get a what?

MOTHER: A job for God's sake. Get some order into your life and face up to your responsibilities and reality.

ERROL: What reality do you know about, and what responsibilities have I got, you just tell me that?

MOTHER: For a start you've got a responsibility to me.

ERROL: I've got a responsibility to me, just me, so don't come any of this natural law of obedience crap just because you've got a responsibility to me, and it's tough innit, but that's the Catch-22 of having kids. You're in it up to your neck and you stand or fall by my moral standards. *(Pause.)* I mean, what do you want me to do? Go work for the CRE? Join the police? Stand for Parliament? Or perhaps you want me to make a bid for Trevor McDonald's job and spend the whole day talking shit on the television!

MOTHER: Your reality, Errol, is that girl, and your duty, your responsibility is to look after her, to help her instead of yourself.

ERROL: Utter crap.

MOTHER: Jesus! –

ERROL: – was a white boy and I'm a black boy so don't give me no broken images to worship.

MOTHER: You just tell me what you lazy bastards are doing over and above giving black people a bad name.

ERROL: We're on the march. Africa.

MOTHER: Talk sense, Errol. How the hell are you going to get to Africa, swim? You've got an overdraft the size of the

37

national debt and as long as you sit on your arse talking shit it's going to grow. That's reality. I don't know what kind of economics they taught you, son, but the basics are clear to any fool to see.

ERROL: *(More controlled now.)* What do you know about seeing? Even your own next-door neighbour, who can only just about do subtractions, knows more than you. If my dad was alive he wouldn't take all this crap from you or them sitting down.

MOTHER: How the hell do you know? Come on, tell me how you know he wouldn't take all this 'crap' you say is going around.

ERROL: Because he wouldn't, that's how I know. He's my dad, no man, no black man can stand by and take all this crap.

MOTHER: Errol, listen. What are you talking about? What are you fighting? Tell me, I'd like to know.

ERROL: Tell you shit!

MOTHER: You're driving yourself mad, son. You'll have a breakdown.

ERROL: Have a what?

MOTHER: A breakdown. You're putting too much pressure on yourself.

ERROL: *(Laughs out loud.)* Pressure! I'm putting too much pressure on myself...

MOTHER: Look. Errol, why don't you just have a talk with Alvin tomorrow, eh? If you can't talk to me then for God's sake have a word with your brother. I can't sit by and take this much longer, okay?

ERROL: Alvin and I have plans, Mother, that don't include you.

MOTHER: Errol, listen…

ERROL: And when this strike is over we're going to strike again. Yeah, that's it. Two strikes in one by Alvin and Errol Marshall. A study in economic realignment. That's my new black theory of economics that any fool can see, if only they're black enough that is. *(Pause.)* Mother, why don't you put on your Johnny Mathis LP?

(He goes upstairs with the parcel he came in with tucked under his arm. MOTHER just stares at him as he leaves. He doesn't pull the curtain behind him. She is visibly worried. The back door opens and shuts.)

VERNICE: You still home? *(She enters.)* Girl, it must be you going deaf. You not hear me?

MOTHER: Yes, I heard you.

VERNICE: Is it Alvin? Something's happened? What is it?

MOTHER: Nothing. Nothing. What do you want?

VERNICE: Me jus' come round to tell you…

(ERROL comes downstairs in the same clothes, but apparently ready to go out for the night. He has left the parcel upstairs.)

Lord, what make you decide to come back so soon from wherever it is you spend your time?

ERROL: I'm off out.

VERNICE: No sooner you come back as you take up you all backside again. Me ain't know what the hell yer do with you all time.

ERROL: We plan.

VERNICE: Plan, me arse. Only planning you all do is where yerall going get you next spliff from. You still walking out the white girl?

ERROL: Shelley?

VERNICE: Is she who I mean.

ERROL: On and off.

VERNICE: She alright, I suppose. Betta than mosta them. What you think?

ERROL: Scrubber. Boring scrubber at that.

VERNICE: Well look the hell. The boy bad. He swear like a trooper. *(She laughs.)* You better not upset your mother so, you know. Lord. She have enough trouble with you all as it is.

(ERROL sucks his teeth.)

MOTHER: Do you have to go now? I thought you weren't meeting Shelley till eight.

ERROL: I'm walking. After all, we're all going to be walking tomorrow, aren't we?

VERNICE: You just watch yourself, boy, you hear me?

(ERROL smiles at her and goes via the front door.)

Anyhow, Stanley ask me to marry him. That's what me drag meself over here to tell you. When me ring him he jus' ask me straight out on the damn phone when I goin' marry him. You surprise now, ain't you?

MOTHER: And what did you say?

VERNICE: Yes girl, course me goin' marry the man. You don't think me should, or what?

MOTHER: Of course you should, if that's what you want.

VERNICE: Well. I getting on an' I don't think anybody else goin' ask me. Charmain soon goin' leave home an' me can't live on me memories for they all too painful so… So I tell him yes.

MOTHER: I suppose this calls for a drink.

(She gets up and goes across to the cabinet. Pause.)

Vernice, I'm happy for you.

VERNICE: Me arse. You beginning to sound human.

MOTHER: *(Hands her a drink and sits.)* For you both.

VERNICE: Lord!

(They drink.)

MOTHER: Am I the first to know?

VERNICE: Me want to get me hands on Stanley before I going tell anyone else for definite.

MOTHER: That includes Charmain?

VERNICE: Course girl, it includes Charmain.

MOTHER: You mean it's not certain.

VERNICE: Vivien, girl. I know enough men in me time to know that until me feel the ring on this same finger, nothing is definite. I make a fool uh meself enough times over blasted men as it is. Girl, you lucky with having jus' the one man. You ain't waste your time finding out there's no flickin' second chance. Stanley is me last hope.

MOTHER: When will you see him again?

VERNICE: Dinner time is about that time they all crawl round, nuh! *(She laughs.)* Jesus Christ! Why's life so friggin' difficult? Sometimes me feel like jus' packing up me bags an' goin' home. Pickin' off me mango and drinking me rum. Gimme one drink, huh. *(MOTHER pours her a drink.)* Back home if me feel like doin' me own thing I jus' move me arse an' do it an' don't matter what nobody say they goin' think.

MOTHER: It's different now, though.

VERNICE: Fuck me raas different! What you know about different! In all the years you been here girl, you ain't get off you backside to go down the Caribbean Club, let alone get yerself on a boat or a plane to go and see yer own fockin' family. Girl. you better leave you raas where it is for yer sister Vera goin' cut you good if she done see you comin'.

MOTHER: It's not that I didn't want to…

VERNICE: Bollocks. You didn't want to do this and you didn't want to do that. Lord, you goin' get yer lot when you son come back. And that Errol goin' give the white girl he backfoot an' start taking up with his own. Me see it now. He goin' marry black an' there goin' be plenty trouble.

MOTHER: But Vernice, it doesn't make any difference who he chooses to marry.

VERNICE: Girl, you think too white. *(She helps herself to another drink.)*

MOTHER: What's that supposed to mean? *(VERNICE sucks her teeth.)* Has Charmain got a boyfriend?

VERNICE: Charmain ain't got no boyfriend, girl. She too funny, so and high an' mighty, but when she do I tell you she goin' take up black. Me ain't want no breeds in me family.

MOTHER: Vernice, that's not right.

VERNICE: Lemme tell you. Remember back home at school an' we all use to sit on the beach an' thing an' ask each other if we goin' marry a white man if he ask us, an' how we all say no, we ain't goin' marry no fockin' white. Well today, me arse, them all sitting on they backside asking each other what they goin' do if a black man ask them, and the same with the boys them. What they goin' do if it come they want to marry a black girl.

MOTHER: Rubbish!

VERNICE: Backside, you ain't know the boy. He ain't a child now, you know, and he…

MOTHER: Vernice, do you really wish you were back home?

I mean, would you go tomorrow if you could?

(Pause. They look at each other. VERNICE looks away.)

VERNICE: Me ain't know. I goin' drop off the kettle tomorrow when Stanley bring it round. I hope I goin' find you here you know.

(VERNICE goes via the kitchen. MOTHER, now alone, looks around. She doesn't really want to sit on her own but she has no choice now. She goes back to sit down but is on edge. She gets up and goes into the kitchen for ALVIN's clothes. She comes back through with them, plus an iron. She sets up the ironing board and everything, but can't be bothered to do it just yet. She gets out the photograph album and moves to sit down. She pours herself a drink and opens the album as the lights go down.)

SCENE TWO

Lights up. It is turned midnight. We hear ERROL and SHELLEY coming in the front door. ERROL comes into the front room first, but is closely followed by SHELLEY. She goes to sit and ERROL throws off his jacket onto the back of the settee. He moves across to go upstairs.

SHELLEY: Where you off?

ERROL: I'm off for a piss, you wanna come?

SHELLEY: No, I just wondered, that's all.

(ERROL goes. SHELLEY takes off her coat and sees to her face in the mirror. She hears him coming back so she quickly rushes back to her seat as if she hasn't moved. ERROL comes in and shuts the door, pulling the curtain across it.)

She isn't awake, is she?

ERROL: Who?

(He goes to the cabinet, deciding what drink to have.)

SHELLEY: You know who. Your mum.

ERROL: Don't know. What d'you wanna drink?

SHELLEY: Anything really, I'm not bothered. *(Pause.)* What is there?

ERROL: You asked for 'anything really' so that's what you've got now.

(He hands her a drink.)

SHELLEY: Thanks. Cheers.

(ERROL sucks his teeth.)

I see she finished off Alvin's stuff before she went to bed.

ERROL: Shit. She did 'n' all.

(He goes to the pile of ironed clothes in the corner.)

SHELLEY: I feel sorry for her.

ERROL: *(Picking it up.)* See this dashiki?

SHELLEY: This what?

ERROL: This shirt.

SHELLEY: Yeah.

ERROL: Alvin's gonna give it to me when he gets back 'cos he's buying one out there. He's gonna bring us some beads too.

SHELLEY: That'd be nice.

ERROL: What?

SHELLEY: I said that'd be nice.

ERROL: *(Mimicking.)* 'That'd be nice.' Have you seen his shades?

SHELLEY: No, I don't think so.

ERROL: No, you wouldn't have I don't suppose. Do you wanna?

SHELLEY: If you like.

ERROL: Here. He keeps them in here in the back of this drawer.

(He finds them and puts them on.)

SHELLEY: Is that 'em?

ERROL: No, it's a packet of Tampax I've got strapped to me head or didn't you notice?

SHELLEY: I've never seen him wearing them so how am I supposed to know that they're the ones? Anyhow, I've seen some like them before. Did he get 'em from Woolies?

ERROL: Woolies? You've never seen anyone wearing these, or any like 'em. These specs aren't for wearing. He got 'em off a Black American GI who knew Huey Newton. They're Huey Newton's dark glasses. Genuine Panther specs.

SHELLEY: Really? You mean Black Panthers have worn them?

ERROL: I just said so, didn't I?

SHELLEY: I know, but I'd never have believed it just to look at them.

ERROL: You what? *(He puts them away sharply.)* You don't know what the fuck you're on about half the time, do you? Well answer me. Do you?

(She looks like she is going to start crying.)

Oh for fuck's sake, I might as well talk to the wall.

(He goes for another drink.)

SHELLEY: Sorry.

ERROL: What you sorry for?

SHELLEY: I don't know. I'm just sorry, that's all.

ERROL: Jesus!

(Long pause.)

SHELLEY: Errol.

ERROL: Yeah, that's me. I'm still here remember?

SHELLEY: I think…

ERROL: Well, go on then. Quit the Hitchcock suspense stuff, will you?

SHELLEY: I think I'm going to have to leave home after my exams.

ERROL: So?

SHELLEY: You can't just say 'so', it's important.

ERROL: Okay then. For fuck's sake, why have you got to leave home?

SHELLEY: I don't know.

ERROL: Brilliant. Well, what do you want me to do? Go and ask the FBI to investigate, because I've got a hotline to J. Edgar Hoover upstairs if you're interested. I'll just go give him a buzz shall I?

(He moves to go upstairs.)

SHELLEY: But it's serious.

ERROL: Course it's serious. It's so fucking serious you don't know what the hell you're on about. You might have to leave home but you don't know why! You must think I'm a fucking idiot. Well? Simple really, isn't it. Your wonderful parents can't handle the idea of their virginal lily-white maiden possibly falling prey to the lascivious clutches of an old black ram. *Othello*, page sixty-one or whatever. Well? Come on. They remember when this area was Cortina-country. You know, all kippers and curtains or whatever, don't they?

SHELLEY: He's a motherfucker.

ERROL: Who's a motherfucker? Othello? I think you've got the wrong classical 'O' there. No doubt you'll find Oedipus is your man, if you bothered to pay any attention to what people tell you instead of daydreaming your way through life.

SHELLEY: My dad. He's a motherfucker.

ERROL: Your dad?

SHELLEY: Yes.

ERROL: *(Laughs.)* Look, you can't call your dad a motherfucker.

SHELLEY: Why not? You say it.

ERROL: 'Cos your dad is a motherfucker. That's why you're
here, right, brain of Britain. Jesus. *(Takes it slowly.)*
In theory he has at some point fucked your mother,
i.e. motherfucker.

SHELLEY: I'm sorry.

ERROL: What you sorry about now? Well?

SHELLEY: I don't know.

ERROL: Oh, I see, you don't know again. Shall I change
the record?

SHELLEY: I'm sorry about calling my dad a motherfucker.

ERROL: Oh, I see. I think a 'mindless ugly little redneck
bastard' would be a fairer description. Well? Is that all?

SHELLEY: I don't know where I'm going to.

ERROL: You could enrol at Madame Sheila's on Rose Street
as a hostess. Give us a massage from time to time.

SHELLEY: Is that all you think of me? Is that all you think
I'm worth?

ERROL: Oh bollocks. I was only kidding.

SHELLEY: Well, it's not funny. I don't think it's funny at all.

ERROL: Alright I'm sorry. What do you want? Some kind of
twenty-one-gun salute 'cos your redneck fucking old man's
kicking you out?

(He goes for a drink.)

SHELLEY: I've been thinking…

ERROL: Go on. I'm intrigued.

SHELLEY: Well, maybe we could get a place and…

ERROL: Now I'm amused.

SHELLEY: Why?

ERROL: Oh, come off it.

SHELLEY: It's over two years now, Errol. What do you want from me? I've got feelings too, you know. You can't just go on treating me like dirt.

ERROL: Who's treating you like dirt?

SHELLEY: You are. You never take any notice of anything I say. I might as well not bother, I might as well blend into the wallpaper for all you care. Don't you love me anymore?

ERROL: Don't I what?

SHELLEY: Don't you love me anymore? Have you gone off me?

ERROL: When did I say I loved you?

SHELLEY: Errol!

ERROL: Well, that was ages ago and…

SHELLEY: For a girl it's never ages ago, it's always in her mind. *(Pause.)* I only let you because you…

ERROL: …Bollocks!

SHELLEY: I did! You said that you'd never felt like this before and it was special and…

ERROL: *(Stands.)* Fucking hell! I must have had a few beers.

SHELLEY: Errol, you can't just leave me now, you know. You can't just ditch me like that. You've got responsibility. You owe me something.

ERROL: Owe you what? I owe you shit.

SHELLEY: How can you say that, Errol? After everything I've put up with. After I get used to being just a source of amusement for you and your spars, or whatever you call them. Just a good joke. After I get used to you not talking to me, and when you do it's just to tell me how stupid I am. After I even get used to you screwing those fourth-formers round the back of the club. Yeah, you thought I didn't know, but I'm not stupid, I'm not as stupid as all that and it's them that belong down Rose Street, not me. You owe me something. You've got to look after me, Errol. Please, you've got to look after me.

ERROL: I've got my own plans and they don't include you.

SHELLEY: But they must. They have to…

ERROL: Why? You think you're special, don't you? You think you're somebody really special don't you, just 'cos I've been knocking about with you for a bit.

SHELLEY: Doesn't it mean something to you? After two years it must do, Errol.

ERROL: Yeah. It means you're probably a good screw, which as a matter of fact you aren't. You're just regular, that's all.

SHELLEY: What, you mean just when you need me.

ERROL: That's right.

SHELLEY: A quick one in the bog at the club, or round here when your mum's at work.

ERROL: Don't forget the shop doorways. You were always at your best standing up.

SHELLEY: And that's all I am to you.

ERROL: If you put it like that.

SHELLEY: You're a bastard sometimes.

ERROL: Oh piss off, woman.

SHELLEY: I don't deserve this, Errol, I deserve better.

ERROL: Don't make me laugh, pasty-face. Only two parts of a man's body a woman understands, and if you don't shut up I'm gonna belt your fucking face in with this, understand, my number-two weapon. *(He clenches his fist and there is a long pause.)*

SHELLEY: Don't you have any respect left for me?

ERROL: Shall I tell you what you and others like you deserve? Shall I tell you what you are? You're finished. You thought you could push us around, didn't you? Didn't you?

SHELLEY: I don't understand, Errol.

(Throughout the speech he challenges her both vocally and physically.)

ERROL: There's a phrase. Malcolm used it: 'Chickens coming home to roost.'

SHELLEY: Errol.

ERROL: In your case it means you don't control shit anymore. You don't control the land, the money or the mind. Now you're the tool and we're the craftsmen. Look around the world. Suddenly you're all frightened. There are more black Prime Ministers than white ones. There are more black people than white people. You're a minority – a sickening minority at that. Your economy is all to fuck so what do you do? You try and kick out those of us who are already here and stop anyone else from coming in. Well, it ain't fucking working, is it? We're a beautiful people, a talented, resourceful, strong, dark people, a people just waking up. We're growing and you're scared shitless. Look at yourselves. You need us, you bastards. You need to control us. We've wheedled our way into the main artery of your fucked-up economic system. You can't kick us out like Hitler did to the Jews 'cos if you want to play at being Nazis we ain't your fuckin' jewboys. In the next two days you and others like you will see what you really are. To you all reality is just a game, but to us it's fucking survival, it's pressure, and what fucking pressure do you all know, sticking your ugly heads in the sand? We're gonna show you some reality. Let's see you hold down some pressure. You're so fucking short-sighted you make me laugh. We are here because you were there. The chickens are coming home to roost. That's all you are to me – a historical phenomenon.

(He begins to strut around, squawking – he's doing the 'funky chicken'. He repeats the last sentence, taunting her with it. She just watches him helplessly. After a few moments MOTHER comes downstairs and looks on. She has got out of bed. She wears her dressing gown and slippers.)

Oh hello, mother. We're just playing. Honest, that's all.

(He carries on.)

MOTHER: I don't know what the hell kind of playing you call this, but I thought you'd left all that kind of nonsense behind with the train sets and cowboys and Indians. Why don't you grow up?

ERROL: *(Stops.)* What for?

MOTHER: Shelley, are you alright dear?

SHELLEY: Yes, Miss.

ERROL: Why don't you call her Mrs Marshall, or Ma'am, or God or something? 'Yes, Miss!'

MOTHER: Have you been drinking, Errol?

ERROL: Camels don't need to drink to get high. They just stand up.

MOTHER: Look, it's getting on Errol, and I've got to…

ERROL: Yeah, go on.

MOTHER: I've got to get some sleep. Shelley, as it's late you can sleep here on the settee if you like. Give your parents a ring and tell them if you decide you want to.

SHELLEY: It'll be alright thanks, but I'll have to get back 'cos I've got school tomorrow.

ERROL: Yeah, what a drag. We're having a quiet day in. Some kind of strike or summat on. Don't know if you've heard about it?

MOTHER: Well, I don't mind if you put on some records or something but please try to keep the noise down. People are trying to sleep.

SHELLEY: We're sorry.

MOTHER: It's okay, Shelley.

ERROL: It's okay, Shelley. It's my tits she's getting on.

MOTHER: Goodnight, and don't forget to lock up behind you when you come up.

(She goes.)

ERROL: Goodnight.

SHELLEY: Please, Errol. You should treat her better. She's your mother.

ERROL: I wondered who it was standing there. I knew I'd seen her somewhere. *(Pause.)* Oh, come off it, Shelley. Let's forget it, eh love?

SHELLEY: Forget what?

ERROL: You know. Argument and everything. I'm just playing.

SHELLEY: But Errol.

ERROL: But Errol, nothing. You fancy a cup of tea?

SHELLEY: Yeah, okay.

ERROL: Okay, I'll get it.

(He gets up and goes into the kitchen.)

SHELLEY: Do you want a hand?

ERROL: No. I've just got to put the water in the pan, that's all. Bloody kettle's knackered. It won't be a minute.

SHELLEY: Can't you fix it?

ERROL: Fix what?

SHELLEY: The kettle.

ERROL: Fix it!

SHELLEY: Well, I thought you might be able to adjust something.

ERROL: *(Comes through.)* I'm an Economist and Revolutionary. What the fuck am I supposed to know about electric kettles?

SHELLEY: Nothing, I suppose.

ERROL: Well, there you are then.

SHELLEY: Errol?

ERROL: What now? You want me to fix in some double glazing for you, or maybe you think I ought to refit the carpet whilst the kettle's boiling?

SHELLEY: No. What I wanted to say was, what do you want to do?

ERROL: What kind of question is that?

SHELLEY: Well, what's your ambition, you know? Your goal.

ERROL: I don't have ambition or goal. I have destiny.

SHELLEY: Well, it's the same thing, isn't it?

ERROL: In a word, no.

SHELLEY: What is it, then?

ERROL: Hang on.

(He goes back into kitchen.)

I'm having a Red Stripe.

SHELLEY: Can I have one too?

ERROL: You said you wanted tea.

SHELLEY: I'll have both. It'll help to calm me down.

ERROL: Or loosen up, more like. One cup of tea and a Red Stripe coming up.

(He comes through.)

SHELLEY: Thanks, Errol.

ERROL: Not at all, Miss.

SHELLEY: Can I put an album on? One of those I brought round for you to play?

ERROL: Let's have a look at them first.

SHELLEY: You won't like them.

ERROL: Well, what the fuck did you bring them round for?

SHELLEY: I thought we might listen to them.

ERROL: Even though I don't like them. Well? *(He sucks his teeth.)* You don't listen to the fuckin' lyrics, anyway.

SHELLEY: Well, I…

ERROL: Let's have a look at them.

(SHELLEY gets them.)

Oh my God! I might have guessed. These fuckin' mixed bands are a disgrace! It's only one step better yet they're all too fucking stupid to realise it. What we want is black bands. Black producers and arrangers and black singers to do their own thing. Black businessmen means black music.

SHELLEY: But there isn't any Tamla Motown in England, so how are you going to get all of these things.

ERROL: There's Eddy Grant.

SHELLEY: Who?

ERROL: He does it on his own. He does it all. He lives on the frontline and he's a…he's a…

SHELLEY: He's a what?

ERROL: He runs his own show – does his own thing – entrepreneur. Black entrepreneur. Uses black capital like Berry Gordy.

SHELLEY: I've never heard of him.

ERROL: He's an example, that's what he is. An example of something. *(Pause.)* Take them away and come back here next to me.

(She gets up and puts the albums back. She comes and sits down next to him again.)

My destiny is that of a leader. A leader, do you understand?

SHELLEY: Yeah, I know. I thought that's what you wanted to be. You can do it you know, Errol. *(Pause.)* You're always saying your destiny's to be free, aren't you?

ERROL: The promised land. Freedom of spirit and mind. Freedom of body and action. Do you understand?

SHELLEY: I understand. I see. *(Pause.)* Why don't you kiss me, Errol, if it makes you feel free?

ERROL: Alvin too. Co-leaders. Tomorrow there'll be a Patriotic Front in Britain.

SHELLEY: Hold me, Errol.

ERROL: Tomorrow the sun comes up on a sunken kingdom. An Empire in ruins.

SHELLEY: Don't leave me, Errol. Please.

ERROL: An Empire that's fallen. In the whole history of the world there is no Empire, not even the Roman Empire, that has not come crashing down.

SHELLEY: Errol.

ERROL: And do you know what brought them down – all of them?

SHELLEY: Please Errol.

ERROL: The lust for freedom.

SHELLEY: Please.

ERROL: No man has been more systematically denied his freedom than the black man. Our day is coming. The seeds will soon be plants and the plants will begin to bear forth fruit. *(He turns to SHELLEY.)* And you, all of you, did the sowing.

SHELLEY: Errol, love me.

ERROL: Take them off.

SHELLEY: Yes.

(She begins to take off her tights and pants.)

ERROL: Quick. *(He begins to fumble at his jeans. They begin to make love on the settee.)*

SHELLEY: Errol, Errol.

ERROL: Faster. You sowed, now work, work, work!

SHELLEY: Oh, Errol, this is your destiny. I'm doing it for you, it's for you, just for you.

ERROL: Oh fuck. Fuck, oh, oh! *(He reaches a climax, whilst she still wants more as he does so. After the stillness he comes through and she still wants more. He pushes her off and zips up.)* You'd better go now.

SHELLEY: Errol!

ERROL: It's getting late and you've got to go to school tomorrow, remember.

SHELLEY: You can't. Not again, Errol. Not again.

ERROL: Look, it's late, okay. *(She begins to cry as he picks up the phone and starts to dial for a taxi.)* Can I have a cab please at 201 Crawley Terrace…yes…to Elm Park Estate…just one…five minutes, okay. It'll be here in five minutes.

(Long pause.)

SHELLEY: Errol, I know where my dad's got some money hidden. We could be leaders together, direct our own destiny if that's what you want.

ERROL: What the fuck is this? I don't believe it. You're trying to buy me now.

SHELLEY: I'm not, Errol.

ERROL: How much do you think I cost, then? Three necklaces and a string of plastic beads? Or perhaps just a piece of shiny glass.

SHELLEY: He's got about five hundred pounds under his bed. He doesn't trust banks and I know I can get it while he's out and then we can...

ERROL: I know. We can get ourselves set up in a flat when you get chucked out for insisting on fucking with a nigger. Well?

SHELLEY: We could go away.

ERROL: Where to?

SHELLEY: Couldn't I come to Africa with you?

ERROL: Do me a favour. I don't need no fucking white woman to dangle on a string to show I'm free. I don't need no colour television or white sports car either. When I get off that plane in Africa, you know what I'm gonna do? I'm gonna walk barefoot down the steps onto the tarmac, and kiss the ground like that white cunt, the Pope. I'm gonna sit out in the sun all day listening to the drums till I'm as black as coal. I'm gonna sit there and feel fine 'cos everywhere I turn they'll be as black as me. I'll find myself a family, a new family. Can't I take you to Africa with me! Put your fucking clothes on and watch you don't mess up the woman's settee, you raas clart.

(He pours himself a drink as SHELLEY starts to put on her tights and pants. There is a noticeable lull then SHELLEY speaks up.)

SHELLEY: Is it all over then, Errol? Is that what you're trying to tell me because…

ERROL: Woman, don't ask me such fockin' damn fool questions. Jus' put on yer clothes, nuh. The man goin' come at any moment.

SHELLEY: Can I see you tomorrow afternoon?

ERROL: *(Sucks his teeth.)* Me got me plans to sort out with Alvin.

SHELLEY: But I need to see you tomorrow afternoon.

(Sound of car horn.)

ERROL: You ain't needing nothing but one good bath.

SHELLEY: I want to see you tomorrow, please. Please.

ERROL: Girl, you keeping the man waiting.

SHELLEY: Please, Errol. Please.

(She starts to get hysterical. ERROL puts down his drink and hits her across the face.)

ERROL: You going wake up the focking woman again, you hear me. Get your focking records and go.

(SHELLEY crosses and picks them up. She stares at him then moves towards the door. She has a last desperate attempt. She turns.)

Go! And shut the door behind your arse, nuh, raas!

(The car horn sounds again. SHELLEY leaves. ERROL is on edge. He pours a drink down himself.)

(Lights down.)

END OF ACT ONE

Act Two

SCENE ONE

Lights up. Tuesday: 6.30 a.m.

MOTHER comes downstairs in her dressing gown and slippers. She is carrying an alarm clock, which she places on the sideboard. She picks up her sewing basket and some of ALVIN's clothes. She turns on the fire and sits in front of it all huddled up, cold and shivering. Wearily she begins to sew. After a minute or so we hear a light tapping on the kitchen window. At first she is startled, then she realises who it must be. She puts down her work and goes into the kitchen.

MOTHER: Do you know what time it is?

VERNICE: Yes, girl, but I couldn't sleep.

> *(They enter the front room. VERNICE has on her dressing gown and slippers too.)*

MOTHER: Keep it quiet or you'll wake up Errol…

VERNICE: I see you light on so me think me goin' call round an' see if y'alright.

MOTHER: I couldn't sleep.

VERNICE: Neither could I.

MOTHER: I kept hearing noises like…

VERNICE: Like what?

MOTHER: Like drums in the night.

VERNICE: *(Sucks her teeth.)* That be nothin', girl. It jus' be Errol talking to him brothers in Africa. *(She laughs.)*

MOTHER: I was scared, though.

VERNICE: *(Sucks her teeth.)* Fear's the least uh yer problems.

MOTHER: I wish they'd go to church.

VERNICE: Who?

MOTHER: My two.

VERNICE: You make me laugh. To get them kids into church, you must be joking.

MOTHER: Errol told me it's a white man's institution because it deals with the hereafter instead of the now on earth. Only poor people go to church, so he claims.

VERNICE: You ask the boy when he did win the pools. He think he rich or something. Girl, we needed the church then.

MOTHER: I still need it, and I haven't noticed you queuing up for a seat.

VERNICE: Girl, back home we didn't know nothing else, and when we first come here I don't have to tell you where the only place you feel safe is.

MOTHER: No, you don't have to tell me.

VERNICE: Girl, everywhere we turn. 'No coloureds here' an' 'No vacancies for coloureds'. And the kids them callin' at we in the street. 'Nigger whore, fuck off home' an' 'Monkey, monkey show us your tail'. You remember?

MOTHER: Vernice.

VERNICE: You want to ask that boy of yours how he think a coloured woman arriving in this fockin' country with jus' she two children an' no father for them is goin' get along without the church. *(Pause.)* Life's jus' like one long, long journey and you jus' gotta keep jumping up an' over the obstacles, you hear me? Birth, marriage, death of parents, death of friends, divorce, death of husbands, grandchildren you never goin' see, but you jus' gotta keep on jumpin' otherwise you goin' fall flat on you all face.

MOTHER: I'm sick and tired of jumping.

VERNICE: Well, get out the house, nuh, and find yourself somebody.

MOTHER: I've managed so far.

VERNICE: Well, if you don't want to be carried you've got to talk to someone. *(Pause.)* If it wasn't Wilfred it was somebody, girl. Jus' somebody to help me survive. *(Pause.)* Lord, me ain't know how you do it. I thief money for Charmain's uniform and me still fiddling on the social security yet me still poor. Lord, me ain't know what me goin' do if they find out.

(Pause.)

MOTHER: The first time I ever saw snow in England, Vernice. The first time. Have I ever told you?

VERNICE: Jesus!

MOTHER: I remember. I'd just applied for a job as a clerk with the buses. I'd given up the job in the shoe factory. 'My name is Mrs Marshall, not black sambo, my name is Mrs Marshall, not black sambo, my name is...' and so on. Normal factory job. Alvin was at school. Mrs Teale's class. Errol had whooping cough. I had no money and you and Wilfred had taken Charmain to Bradford to see Wilfred's brother, I think it was. Just before he died. I was alone, as usual, and it was the night before the interview for the clerk's job. I broke into the meter with a nail file. It took me six hours in the dark. All night I filed away as the mice ran about my feet looking for bits of food. Anything at all, scrambling behind the cooker and in the dustbin, in

the bottom of the cupboard, and God knows how, even
on the table top itself. I guess they were hungry too, but
Alvin had beaten them to it. He'd been through all those
places long before they had. It was still dark as the lock
eventually gave way and I pulled out the tray. I pushed
a sixpence back into the meter, turned the dial, and then
discovered that the mice were rats and that there were
only three sixpences left in the tray. Four, when I picked
up the one I'd just put in off the floor. My life savings
amounted to two shillings, and it was stolen money at
that. They said the interview was to be at nine o'clock at
the main depot, so I had four hours to go. I turned out the
lights and sat in the dark again. Then I realised it didn't
matter about saving electricity, for the money just came
back to me and I could put it back in again and so on, so I
put the lights back on. Errol began to cry so I brought him
down and lay him in front of the paraffin heater, hoping
that the fumes would help him sleep. I didn't realise
that they just made his cough worse. The doctor didn't
mention anything about that. When Alvin got up I left the
pair of them and went out to buy some breakfast. I spent
a shilling. I needed a sixpence for the meter and sixpence
for my bus fare to the depot. I'd hoped I'd start that
morning so I didn't leave any change for the return fare.
After they'd eaten, Alvin left for school and I took Errol to
the nursery and told them it was just a bad cough and as
long as they kept him away from the other kids it would
be alright. Well, what else could I do? I needed the job
and only then would I be able to get a proper minder. It
was half past eight. I'd get to the depot just in time. It was
full downstairs so I went upstairs, fighting my way through
the smoke and flat caps till I got to the front. I could feel
the comments and hatred behind me, taste their grimy,
filthy lusting. As we neared the factory gates they all began
to get up and move down the bus. As they did so one of
them began to sing 'Bye, bye, Blackbird' and soon they

were all singing it. I closed my already heavy and swollen eyes and tried to fight back the tears. It wasn't really much good, was it? There's no such thing as getting used to it. If there's one thing I know it's that. I didn't even bother to wipe them away. Perhaps if they saw tears they'd realise I was human. Perhaps not. 'Come on, love. You're just soft. Can't you take a joke?' I shut my eyes even tighter, then I felt a hand on my shoulder. 'Terminus. That'll be fourpence extra. You only paid a tanner.' I opened my eyes. 'Where are we?' I asked. 'Don't you speak English? Terminus. Great Hayton Park. Don't know what you're doing up here.' 'Have I passed the depot?' He sneered at me, then I realised what had happened. I'd fallen asleep and missed the stop. Missed the appointment. I'd just have to be late. 'I'm going back to the depot,' I said. 'Where's your brass then? That'll be eightpence.' I had no money. In that split second of panic I decided to explain. I looked up at him. Sensitive? A sensitive man? Does his daughter play with Alvin at school? Will his grandson marry my granddaughter? 'Get off the bus, nigger, and walk. I'm not taking any of you liver-lipped lot, whether you've got the money or not. Well, move on or there'll be another Notting Hill riot right here.' Did his grandfather own my grandfather? I began to walk but the houses all looked so big, they all looked the same and all the streets even seemed to have the same cars parked on them. The same little dogs played in the garden and the same hands pulled the children back from the gate as I passed. I'd walked in a circle. I was lost. I opened a gate and knocked at a door. I saw the curtain move but I had to ask. A woman of my age opened the door except she was white. 'Excuse me please, but which is the way back to town, please?' No answer. 'Excuse me please?' She spat in my face and my stomach rushed into my mouth as I was sick. She screamed and a man ran out and punched me in the face. He dragged me out of the gate, onto the pavement, and threw me onto the grass verge. I continued to be sick. No food, just bile. Green and white slime. Then it began to snow. I'd never seen snow before but I'd always thought that when it did snow – when I did get to England and see snow – it would be the happiest moment of my life. Nature's most beautiful costume and I'd never seen it. I wet my pants and shivered.

(Long pause.)

VERNICE: Lord, you ain't tell me this before, Vivien.

MOTHER: I don't know. It's not important.

(She gets up and goes to pour herself a drink.)

VERNICE: *(Sucks her teeth.)* You'd come to the wrong country.

MOTHER: No. Not me. I was on the right island. I'd been reading the wrong books. Listening to lies.

VERNICE: It was the truth, then, you know. Back home.

MOTHER: I don't know what they want. Blood?

VERNICE: Who?

MOTHER: Everybody. All of them. My children.

VERNICE: Charmain's already had mine. If Stanley don't say he goin' marry me she only goin' have the bones left to chew.

MOTHER: Don't you ever feel like you're losing touch?

VERNICE: Lord, sometimes me feel like me ain't ever been in touch to start with. Me better go an' see if the girl's alright.

MOTHER: I'll see you later. *(VERNICE gets up.)* Vernice?

VERNICE: Girl, I hear you. You better put away that rum, you hear.

(She goes, leaving MOTHER alone for a few moments. The alarm clock goes off. She gets up and switches it off, then hesitates. She picks it up and goes upstairs to get dressed.)

(Lights down.)

SCENE TWO

Lights up. Early afternoon of the same day.

ERROL comes downstairs carrying a cardboard box of what looks like papers and assorted rubbish. His hair is still uncombed and he has nothing on his feet. His shoes and socks are in the box. He turns on the radio for a time-check, then goes into the kitchen to see if MOTHER is there. He comes out. The radio says it's one o'clock. He turns it off because it's news time. He goes into the kitchen and we hear him putting on the pan for some water to boil up. He comes back into the room and sits. He puts on his shoes and socks. He checks that SHELLEY didn't make a mess on the settee last night by rubbing his hand over it and smelling it. Nothing, so he licks it. Then he starts to take the stuff out of the box. He unfolds a huge sheet of folded paper and we see it has on it drawings of roads. He puts it on the floor, having made enough room for it by pushing back the settee a little. The sheet of paper is a ground plan, which also has arrows and stickers on it. Onto the plan he places cardboard cut-outs of buildings, which he takes from the box. He completes the design with strategically placed toy cars. He gets out a pencil and draws a few arrows, only to rub them out and think. The water's boiling, so he goes through and comes back with a cup of coffee. He's just settling down to work again when he hears VERNICE calling out. He scrambles to get everything back into the box and pushes it under the settee. Enter VERNICE, carrying a kettle.

VERNICE: Morning!

ERROL: It's afternoon.

VERNICE: *(Sucks her teeth.)* After one, for your information.

ERROL: I know.

VERNICE: Well, ain't you got 'morning' in your dictionary?

ERROL: Afternoon.

VERNICE: You jus' get up?

ERROL: No… Yeah.

VERNICE: No, yeah, me arse. Boy you look rough. You out with the white girl, shufflin' your foot last night?

ERROL: Yeah.

VERNICE: All you all don't know how to move yer arse any more Lord, back home we move so. Even you all mother move sheself. *(She demonstrates.)*

ERROL: Well, it was easy for you lot. All you had to do was listen to the bongos, wasn't it? What's that for?

VERNICE: Come again?

ERROL: That?

VERNICE: Oh, this you talking about? You put it under you bed at night to pee in if you all too lazy to get outa bed, what you think it for? Boy, it's a kettle.

ERROL: Yeah, alright, I know it's a kettle, but what's it doing here? Is it for us?

VERNICE: Me ring up Stanley yesterday and ask him if he can bring me round a spare kettle for me remember long time ago he say he have one. He bring me this ordinary cooker kettle around an' telling me it better than electric kettle for it work on gas too. *(Sucks her teeth.)*

ERROL: He's a prat.

VERNICE: Anyhow, here it is. I goin' make meself a quick cuppa with it.

(She goes into the kitchen. ERROL pushes the box further out of sight.)

ERROL: Vernice.

VERNICE: Me hear you.

ERROL: How come he's working today?

VERNICE: Well, he has to, otherwise he'll lose his customers and his round. Or so the man tell me when he drop off the kettle, an' it make a bita sense me suppose.

ERROL: But that's the whole point. To show them that we don't need them. We don't care. They need us.

VERNICE: *(Coming back through.)* But Stanley's already essential. He knows that.

ERROL: Essential to who?

VERNICE: To everyone in the area. The community.

ERROL: What if everyone decided to do that, eh? What about me mother? You could say the same for her 'n' all couldn't you, but you don't.

VERNICE: Child, don't vex me up so. Is you who always talking about serve the community and serve that so here is a big chance to do some serving on your own doorstep.

ERROL: I talk about serving a people, not a community.

VERNICE: I don't care who the hell you talking about serving, but why the hell you not come round and help Charmain? According to your mother she ain't doing the work.

ERROL: Well, you know why she don't do any work, don't you? It's 'cos she spends half the day wandering the streets and sitting in the park. She isn't stupid.

VERNICE: She doesn't know anything about Stanley.

ERROL: Don't be stupid. Course she does.

VERNICE: Know what?

ERROL: Everything. Why don't you just come out into the open with it? It'd probably be the best thing.

VERNICE: You really think so…?

ERROL: Course. Just tell her.

VERNICE: I was going to today but now he's…

ERROL: Now he's what?

VERNICE: Nothing much. I'll ring him tonight.

ERROL: It's truth not tuition that we need, Vernice.

VERNICE: Someone at the door, nuh?

ERROL: Shit, it's probably Alvin.

VERNICE: What, so soon? I thought your mother say he ain't coming till after three.

ERROL: Well, that's what I thought but…

(Enter ALVIN with a large suitcase and a large flight bag. He is twenty-four, slim and slightly taller than ERROL; casually but tidily dressed, with his hair cut closely but neatly. He wears a gold signet ring on his right hand and a thin gold chain around his neck, visible because of his open collar. He is too casual to be important, yet too smart to be bullied in the streets by the police – at least on a first glance.)

Hey man, what's happening?

ALVIN: Hey man, what's happening with you!

ERROL: Alright, the prodigal son!

(They slap hands, US fashion.)

VERNICE: *(Comes through with her drink.)* Well, look the hell. Son of Africa decide to come home.

ALVIN: How you doing, Vernice?

VERNICE: Me fine, but how come you get back so damn quick? I hope you ain't catch no bus nor train for this one goin' give you some licks if you break up the strike.

ERROL: We have ways of making you walk!

ALVIN: No, I met someone on the plane who gave me a lift from the airport. Drove a Scimitar.

VERNICE: A what?

ALVIN: Scimitar. You know, Reliant. Sports car.

VERNICE: Me jus' hope the man black. *(Sucks her teeth.)* You want tea?

ALVIN: Yeah. That'd be great, thanks.

(She goes into the kitchen.) How you doing, man?

ERROL: I-rey. I-rey.

ALVIN: Alright.

ERROL: Jesus, man. We weren't expecting you for at least another hour or so.

ALVIN: Complaining?

ERROL: No, course not. Just great. Great.

ALVIN: *(Inspecting the place.)* That's the way it is. *(Pause.)* Christ, man. Nothing much changes around here, does it?

ERROL: Raas man. Babylon will fall, give it time, me brother. All I and I need is a little time fe we survive.

VERNICE: *(Coming back with a cup of tea.)* Boy, what happen to all you hair, nuh?

ERROL: Yeah. What happened?

ALVIN: What do you mean, what happened?

VERNICE: Look the hell! What happened, nuh? *(She sits down.)*

ERROL: You come a baldhead, nuh. And all this gold and thing. I thought you throw them away. You never use to wear them before.

ALVIN: Well…

VERNICE: Well what, me arse. The boy gone an' find himself some pretty black girl with plenty money. Is right?

ERROL: Hey!

ALVIN: Come on. I just wanted to get it cut for the funeral and everything.

VERNICE: Boy, you pants tight so it looks like something goin' give way. Is how they wearing things now?

ALVIN: I suppose so. I don't really know.

ERROL: Hey, have you got jet lag? What's it like?

ALVIN: Yeah. I'm a bit knackered.

VERNICE: Ain't no aeroplane finish the boy off, I tell you. He been spending too much time messin' up the girls them.

ERROL: Yeah, I bet.

VERNICE: Boy, you looking good, though. You raas clart man, you looking fine you know. You might even say that for once you got you all black backside looking respectable.

ALVIN: *(Sarcastic.)* Why, I thank you both. Nice of you to say so.

(VERNICE sucks her teeth.)

ERROL: Raas!

(They slap hands again.)

VERNICE: How all you family then? You get on with them?

ALVIN: Sort of.

ERROL: What d'you mean, sort of?

ALVIN: Well, they're a funny lot, you know.

VERNICE: Boy, I hope you ain't come none uh that college shit with you people, for they goin' think you come jus' like you all mother.

ALVIN: Nothing like that.

ERROL: You bet. You probably told them there were elephants in Piccadilly Circus.

ALVIN: Don't be a prick.

VERNICE: No ain't know why the pair of you bother doing any studying for if all you going do is play the arse, nuh.

ERROL: We're studying our own thing now, Vernice. He's got his own brand of politics and I've got my own brand of economics. Boy, what a team! What a team!

VERNICE: What you goin' win?

ERROL: Win?

VERNICE: Why you not get your arse across and teach me child 'steada playing the arse.

ALVIN: Charmain?

ERROL: Flunking out at school.

VERNICE: What you say?

ERROL: Flunking.

VERNICE: Boy, me hope that ain't rude, for if it is I goin' thump you arse one lick.

ALVIN: No, Vernice. It means not doing too well.

ERROL: That's right.

VERNICE: Well, why you not say that?

ERROL: I did in a different way.

VERNICE: You all fockin' education an' the girl strugglin' so. Look, I goin' now but I hope I goin' see you all an' you schoolbooks later on, save me some time an' some friggin' money. *(To ALVIN.)* And I hope you ain't mash up me camera. I expect to see it later on too.

(She exits.)

ERROL: Things getting organised you know, man. They coming together and there be a lotta plans and things we gotta get sorted out if we going link up with the strike an' everything. For a few days me didn't think you going make it back in time, man. I shitting up meself, but then me remember you have you flight book up and everything. Still, plans man, plans.

ALVIN: Hey, hold on, man.

ERROL: What?

ALVIN: Well, just hold it, that's all. You've got to at least give us some time to do some eating and a bit of thinking. God, I'm knackered out, you know.

(ERROL gets up and goes through to the kitchen.)

ERROL: Suppose you used to rice and goat now.

ALVIN: What?

ERROL: Rice and goat. Ram goat liver and thing.

ALVIN: Why?

ERROL: Well, didn't you eat much out there?

ALVIN: Yeah, course I ate.

ERROL: Well, you must have had some rice and goat. What about saltfish and johnny cakes?

ALVIN: Yeah, I see now. Yeah.

ERROL: You know what she's cooked you?

ALVIN: Lemme guess. Could it be…or no, it couldn't be.

ERROL: Go on. Have a shot in the dark.

ALVIN: Er, er…

ERROL: Yes Mr Marshall, Mr Alvin Marshall. For one thousand pounds can you tell me the recipe of the day?

ALVIN: Well, I'm not sure about it but… You've really got me there, Hughie.

ERROL: Oh come now, your time's running out. Five…four… three…two…one…

ALVIN: I've got it! Is it…is it flat meat and two veg?

ERROL: Correct! And here is your delicious first prize in place of the cash advertised. *(He comes through with the food.)* One sumptuous plate of flat meat and two veg with the added delight of one or two potatoes liberally sprinkled around. But hold it a minute. Hold it! Could they possibly be yam in disguise? He goes in a little closer to inspect the evidence only to find that, much to the crowd's astonishment… *(ALVIN catches his breath.)* …they're potatoes.

(ALVIN lets his breath out.)

ALVIN: Cheers.

ERROL: My pleasure.

ALVIN: If you look at the top of that bag... *(Pointing with his knife.)* I've brought summat back for you both, though it ain't much.

ERROL: Raas man! Me best go check it out, nuh.

(He gets up.)

ALVIN: If you want.

ERROL: Raas!

ALVIN: Hey! Don't rip the fucking bag apart.

ERROL: Well, where is it then?

ALVIN: I said, it's at the top.

ERROL: Is it fuck.

ALVIN: It is.

ERROL: Is this hide and seek or something?

ALVIN: Jesus! Look, I'll get it. You're as subtle as a fucking customs officer.

(He moves to get up.)

ERROL: No, I've got it. Is this it?

ALVIN: Yeah. They're both in it.

ERROL: Well one of 'em's a bottle. Is that for me?

ALVIN: Is it fuck.

ERROL: What is it?

ALVIN: Take it out and see.

ERROL: Rum!

ALVIN: Well, she likes it, don't she?

ERROL: A bit, I suppose.

ALVIN: Well, it'll last. It was all I could get through customs. I was gonna try and bring her back some of the white rum in a pop bottle, but I knew they'd rumble that one straight away.

ERROL: If it's the same shit as she got sent over at Christmas, fucking glass'll have melted before you got to England. *(Holds up a wooden Afro comb.)* Is this mine?

ALVIN: Yeah.

ERROL: *(Trying it out.)* It's alright.

ALVIN: It looks like your hair ain't seen a comb in weeks.

ERROL: Just got up, ain't I. It's great. Where'd you get it?

ALVIN: It's African. Check the carving. Done in Yoruba.

ERROL: Where's that?

ALVIN: Africa. I said it's African.

ERROL: Me ain't stupid, you know. Where in Africa, man?

ALVIN: Nigeria.

ERROL: Cool. Them is cool. Craftsmen.

ALVIN: Is this all she cooked?

ERROL: Yeah.

ALVIN: Fuck me. She must think I'm on a diet or something.

ERROL: She's been feeding us for years as if we were both on a fucking diet, or have you just noticed? *(Pause.)* Hey, hang on a minute.

ALVIN: I ain't off nowhere.

ERROL: How come it says 'Made in Hong Kong' on here. You lying bastard.

ALVIN: Oh come off it, man. I told you it's Yoruban. African.

ERROL: Africa fucking Hong Kong, you tight bastard.

ALVIN: No, you're wrong. Let me have a look.

(ALVIN comes across to him.)

ERROL: Here.

ALVIN: I don't see anything. Where's it say Hong Kong?

ERROL: On the other side, jewboy.

ALVIN: Oh dear. Yes, Errol, you're right. Take it back straight away.

ERROL: You cunt, you stuck it on didn't you?

ALVIN: Me? Oh no, not me. Trades Description Act, old boy. I wouldn't be so deceitful. I'll finish this and then take it back to the shop I bought it from.

ERROL: Give us it back, bastard.

ALVIN: That's gratitude for you.

(He gets up and takes his plate through to the kitchen.)

ERROL: Hey, England are getting some more black players in the squad.

ALVIN: About time. How's West Brom doing?

ERROL: Okay, I suppose. They're signing up some new brothers too.

ALVIN: No.

ERROL: What do you mean, no?

ALVIN: Well, what I meant was how are they doing in the league, you know? Results, since I've been away.

ERROL: Not too good. Lost 3-0 to Leeds last week and 4-2 at Palace on Saturday.

ALVIN: *(Comes back through.)* Brilliant!

ERROL: What you on about?

ALVIN: Well, you claim to support this team.

ERROL: So what? Anyhow, how come you ain't talking black?

ALVIN: What?

ERROL: You know. You've been over there for a while now and I thought you might have picked up a bit of the lingo. You know, add a bit of authenticity to the banter.

ALVIN: Oh that lingo. The English language.

ERROL: Shut up, prick! You know what I mean. You ain't come up with a single new 'un yet.

ALVIN: I tell you what I did see though.

ERROL: What?

ALVIN: A rasta football team.

ERROL: Bollocks.

ALVIN: No, I'm tellin' you. The Dreadlocks. AFC Dreadlocks. You know, like AFC Bournemouth. They play in red, green and gold stripes.

ERROL: Are you serious?

ALVIN: When they go up for a header, man, they go up high. Talk about floating about at the far post waiting for a cross.

ERROL: You're bullshitting.

ALVIN: I've got pictures, man. *(Gets up.)* Here, I'll get 'em.
They aren't very good 'cos it's that instant Polaroid thing
that Vernice lent us but you'll see. *(Sits.)* There.

ERROL: Bloody hell! I thought you were bulling me up!
Do they have any crowd trouble?

ALVIN: Are you kidding? By half-time most of the crowd are
asleep, man. By full time they're on a different planet.
It could be fucking ice hockey as far as they knew.

ERROL: God, and that's the harbour, isn't it?

ALVIN: Yeah.

ERROL: What's that?

ALVIN: That's the house we lived in, don't you remember?

ERROL: Yeah, course. Just vaguely.

ALVIN: Bollocks! You were only two when we left.

ERROL: Well, you were hardly a fucking pensioner at five.

ALVIN: But I remember more than you.

ERROL: Did they all remember you?

ALVIN: Most of them.

ERROR: Have you got a picture of me dad's cricket gear
on display?

ALVIN: No.

ERROL: Why not?

ALVIN: It wasn't there.

ERROL: Oh yeah? Someone must know. She said it was on
display in some sort of cabinet in the Civic Hall, what

with him being the first from the island to get selected for the full team.

ALVIN: Yeah I know, but it wasn't there.

ERROL: Someone must have known where it was, didn't you ask?

ALVIN: Course I asked and…

ERROL: And?

ALVIN: And nothing. Our Uncle, her brother, said he thought all that gear had been buried with him, then he pissed off without saying another word. Looked at me like I was mad, or something. *(Pause.)* She was probably just bragging, bullshitting us.

ERROL: She gets on my fucking tits sometimes.

ALVIN: Oh come on, man.

ERROL: 'Oh come on, man,' nothing. You know where she is, don't you?

ALVIN: I had put two and two together, but what d'you expect?

ERROL: You what? You don't know what it's been like living with the big white chief for the last two fucking weeks. You know what she called us all?

ALVIN: Who all?

ERROL: The Black Front.

ALVIN: What?

ERROL: Drug addicts and jigaboos. She's off her fucking head. How do you think I'm gonna feel going down Ram Jams and having to face that lot and tell them that I couldn't even persuade me own mother to join the strike?

ALVIN: They'll understand.

ERROL: Understand what? It's okay for you 'cos you've been off the frontline for a couple of weeks. It's me that's gonna get all the blame.

ALVIN: Everyone knows she's different.

ERROL: Everyone knows she's weak.

ALVIN: Look, it's over with, man. Cool it, okay? Just cool it. We can't do anything about it. It's her y'ought to let burn herself out, not you. It's her problem, right? It happened and it ain't worth arguing about.

ERROL: Okay then. What about the fucking milkman? He's working too.

ALVIN: Who, Stanley?

ERROL: The same. Vernice has just been round talking shit about how he'll lose his whole business if he strikes, and how everyone knows he's essential anyway so what's the point.

ALVIN: And?

ERROL: Essential my arse. If they all want a pint of milk they can go and buy it and all the black people in the area should have the sense already to buy in enough milk for the next two days.

ALVIN: Look, he's got a point.

ERROL: Like fuck.

ALVIN: I'm not sure about the strike myself anymore.

ERROL: Bollocks! You turned white en route, or what?

ALVIN: Look at it logically.

ERROL: Which is how I think I do but go on.

82

ALVIN: We all strike for two days, right?

ERROL: Right.

ALVIN: Buy nothing British, don't go to work, stay off the
transport. In other words, stay out of sight, apart from
those walking to see friends or relatives.

ERROL: Right.

ALVIN: Well, think of this then, and just imagine it. Two old
men sat on a park bench an hour ago, or in two hours'
time or any time tomorrow. One says to the other: 'Just
like the old days, eh? Glad to be rid of the black bastards.'
Other one agrees: 'Aye, pity we can't have this permanent.
You know, all the time. No blacks in sight.' They think
for a while and then one says to the other: 'I suppose
we could, couldn't we?' 'Yeah, we could,' he says back.
'Where do you find the number of the National Front?
Oh, I know. Let's look it up in the white pages.' The pair
of them get up and go off to fucking do something about it.

ERROL: Very funny. Great story. You should be on telly.
Basically, you're jacking out aren't you? You're fucking
scared now.

ALVIN: These two old men, what they don't know is, fuck,
isn't it inconvenient that the buses and the tubes and the
trains are running a reduced service. What they don't
think is, fuck, without the black doctors and nurses in this
country the hospitals face crisis. What they don't think
is, fuck, a few factories have got to shut down production
for a while and the paki-shop isn't open. These aren't
problems to worry about anymore; they're a challenge.
They can, and will, be solved as quickly as possible, even
if it means bringing in the fucking army. Stanley might just
have a point.

ERROL: And you think she might too?

ALVIN: I don't know. Maybe. It's just not that simple, man.

ERROL: Jesus!

(Long pause.)

ALVIN: Have you been out today?

ERROL: I told you, I've only just got up.

ALVIN: Well, look, man, you're going to find out anyway.
The streets are full of black people doing shopping,
buying clothes, newspapers, getting taxis and so on.
It's not working, man. It was never gonna really work.

ERROL: So whose side are you on now, then?

ALVIN: Whose side?

ERROL: You fucking heard!

ALVIN: Mine.

ERROL: And what about the plan; are you frightened of that
too? Well? I've spent four weeks casing that joint and we
ain't gonna get caught if that's what's worrying you. The
plans are right here. Here *(He pulls out the box and begins
to arrange the contents on the floor.)* Four weeks it's taken me
to do all this, right down to how long the traffic lights stay
on red at every junction within half a mile of the bank. It's
practically fucking foolproof and you're jacking!

ALVIN: Who says I am? I never said anything about the job.
I was talking about the strike and why that's jacked itself.

ERROL: You mean you still wanna do the job?

ALVIN: Yeah.

ERROL: Yeah? Just like we planned?

ALVIN: Yeah.

ERROL: I've got the armour upstairs, you know. Two rifles, two pistols like we said. You can't jack now.

ALVIN: I said yeah. I ain't jacking.

ERROL: Thank God for that. I thought you'd turned fucking yellow.

ALVIN: Me?

ERROL: Yes man, you. Boy, you take a lot off me mind. Gimme one drink, nuh. Drinka water.

ALVIN: Okay, cool it, that's all. Just cool it.

(ALVIN goes for a glass of water.)

ERROL: Yeah, okay, man. Okay, but you had me shitless. *(Pause.)* I still think you're full of shit about the strike though. Probably just bad leadership if it's not fully operational, but I guess it'll be alright as long as you don't break it.

(ALVIN comes in and gives him the water.)

ALVIN: Why shouldn't I break it?

ERROL: For fuck's sake, man.

ALVIN: It'll be perfect cover.

ERROL: Come on, man. Everyone from here to the fucking CIA probably knows you're a member of the Black Front.

ALVIN: Reformed member. No threat, no surveillance.

ERROL: Look, what is this shit, man? I thought you were tired?

ALVIN: I am.

ERROL: Well, why the fuck are you pissing me up with all these games, then?

ALVIN: I told you, man. We'll do the job just as I've planned it.

ERROL: Okay, man. I'm sorry.

ALVIN: There'll be one small difference, though.

ERROL: What small difference?

ALVIN: The money.

ERROL: What about the fucking money? I told you we'll take about five thousand minimum.

ALVIN: I want to keep back five hundred.

ERROL: No man, the Black Front needs it all. What do you want go thief five hundred for.

ALVIN: You haven't let me finish.

ERROL: Listen, man. If we donate a sum that size we're soon gonna be running the Black Front anyway, then we can do what we like with the money. Take back a thousand or two thousand or even everything, but why risk the leadership for five hundred! The papers are bound to print how much we take so they'll know we ripped them off.

ALVIN: I want you to take the five hundred and go for a holiday in the Caribbean.

ERROL: Bollocks, you ain't serious. I ain't fucking Ronald Biggs, you know. I stay here and use the money with the Black Front.

ALVIN: It's the only reason I'm doing the job, man. I want you to go home for yourself and see it so I don't have to explain to you why I think different now. I want you to see it with your own eyes, man.

ERROL: Look, if that's all it is I can get hold of a different five hundred tomorrow and piss off, but the job, man. You must do the job for the Black Front and nothing else or it's not right, man.

ALVIN: Where's this five hundred coming from?

ERROL: A friend. No bollocks. I can get it.

ALVIN: Sure?

ERROL: Sure I'm sure.

ALVIN: I mean, can you get it tomorrow? I mean just lay your hands on it?

ERROL: I can get it any time, man.

ALVIN: Right, that's settled then.

ERROL: What's settled?

ALVIN: I'm not doing the job.

ERROL: What the fuck's got into you? You find God over there or something?

ALVIN: You know how we always used to talk about 'truth' and the 'fight'?

ERROL: You mean in those long dim days of the week before last?

ALVIN: Well, what is it man, that West Indians here always mention when they talk about home?

ERROL: Come on, man.

ALVIN: I'll tell you. The weather. The weather, Errol, and picking fucking mangos off a tree. They've been here too long. You know what it's really like, man, and the same will be true in Africa. It's full of all the diseases of decolonisation, which they don't realise has eaten away at their islands in the sun. Inflation, unemployment, political violence – remember them? Fucking weather! And then when I tried to talk to them, our own relatives, not just any black people, you know how they treated me? Like a stranger in a very strange land, and that's how I felt. Alone, man. And they don't see it like we do over here.

ERROL: I'm not surprised they ignored you. Seems like you turned into a white man as you crossed the International Date Line or something. A curious phenomenon of the native son looking down his nose at his own fucking people.

ALVIN: You think I did that? You of all fucking people.

ERROL: Course you did, or why else would they cut you dead? It's too late for me to become a part of the white world, but I notice you're still trying like fuck.

ALVIN: Look man, you'd better decide how much of you is Biko and how much is BSc. Econ. before the shit hits the fan because when it does you're going to have to run somewhere for cover, and if your own family won't give it to you, and there's no refuge in your place of birth, then where the fuck are you gonna go? Well?

ERROL: And which white boy's gonna let you hide behind him? Hang on, I know, I've heard this shit before, on the telly. You're gonna fight for the dispossessed and oppressed of the world, regardless of colour, starting right here in Britain on your own doorstep. Isn't that it? 'Dispossessed and oppressed versus the rest'. Well fuck me!

ALVIN: I'm going to train as…

ERROL: It's just so fucking predictable. A social worker! Three cheers for the community-minded negro.

ALVIN: Look, what the hell were we fighting for?

ERROL: What were we fighting for?

ALVIN: A place in the sun? In Montego Bay or Nairobi perhaps. It's fucking pointless when you've got enough fucking problems sitting on a beach in Brighton without getting your head kicked in by a bunch of bastard Hell's Angels.

ERROL: Well, you fucking explain to them that you're a social worker and not a black man as they get out their crowbars and jacks to mash up your fucking head with.

ALVIN: I'll explain, but I'll stay here and do it, not take up my arse somewhere else and talk shit up to my arse in genuine authentic black poverty.

ERROL: Look Al, man. Is this some kind of stunt you've been thinking up on the plane? Well, come on man. If it is it's worked, okay. Good job. Congratulations and all that. Well? I'm convinced. You fooled me. Hey!

ALVIN: A lot can happen in two weeks.

ERROL: Bollocks, man. Come on, man. Hey!

ALVIN: Errol, I went a third of the way round the world and back. I didn't just go to college for a term, or up to Leicester on an anti-Nazi rally. This was like an explosion in my head, man. It was as if I was seeing all the scaffolding I had built my life on suddenly collapsing, and out of this rubble I had to quickly build up something new otherwise I was finished. I'm not joking. I couldn't talk to them, man. They kept looking at me as if they felt sorry for me, as if I was a victim or something, so what the fuck could I do, man, except drive myself sick with question after question – asking myself stupid fucking questions.

ERROL: So you've decided we're better off here?

ALVIN: Yes, man.

ERROL: We're better off forgetting the strike and the job, we'd best forget we're black – turn the other cheek – settle down and get a fucking job, just sit back and wait, just hang out happy niggers playing ball or talking integration till it happens.

ALVIN: Till what happens?

ERROL: Fucking genocide. Being black isn't a gimmick, you know.

ALVIN: To you it's more a gimmick than you realise. West Brom and black players in the English squad, black talk this, and Africa that, baldhead and arming the community. Jesus, Errol, we've forgotten a lot between us.

ERROL: Forgotten what? You might have forgotten.

ALVIN: Unity, man.

ERROL: How the fuck can I unite with you, uncle? You're the one who's done the forgetting. You've forgotten what it's like to be stopped in the street and searched for no reason. You've forgotten what it's like to be called a nigger by a kid who's barely old enough to talk. You've forgotten what it's like to be beaten up at a football match, and as you lay in the St John's bit hear them all screaming in delight because someone's scored. It's only later that you discover it's the new black centre-forward who's scored. He's not a 'fucking nigger'. Well, not till he gets changed anyway. And you've forgotten why I wear a nine-inch scar on my leg.

ALVIN: Of course I haven't.

ERROL: 'Against the wall motherfucker! What was that boy? I hate you niggers…'

ALVIN: Look man I was there and…

ERROL: 'I'm gonna cut your balls off if I hear another word...'

ALVIN: Errol, for Christ's sake!

ERROL: 'An active buck, eh? Give me his knife, Constable. Wouldn't it be ironic if I used his own knife to cut off his balls. Keep still, nigger, or I'll cut you for real, boy! You black bastard...! Aghhh!'

ALVIN: You sick bastard, shut up! For God's sake shut up!

ERROL: Shut up! Shut up! Shut up! What the fuck do you know now, but shut up! All this crap about your life collapsing and you rebuilding it. You rebuilt nothing bastard, you just collapsed. You bastard!

ALVIN: That's right, I'm a bastard. Vera let that one slip, I've got to question it, man... I've got to find new order...

ERROL: Oh big fucking deal out there. That's a plus for me fucking mother as far as I'm concerned. Fucking white man's morals!

ALVIN: But...

ERROL: But you know nothing! You're finished! You're no more stable than a bleeding spinning top on its last rotation. What about me dad's gear?

ALVIN: I don't know. I told you.

ERROL: What about me dad's grave? I noticed there weren't a picture of that either, even though I asked you for one specially. Didn't they tell you where it was? Well, social worker? Well!

ALVIN: It's unmarked, they said.

ERROL: Unmarked! Filled you with some shit, didn't they? Star fucking West Indian cricketer in unmarked

grave! I'll bet me dad's pissing himself at your initiative.
Bloody disgrace you are! Brush you off with any old shit!
Probably felt sorry for you, all intense and committed.
Couldn't even talk to his own people on their level.
Me dad would puke if he could see you!

ALVIN: And what the fuck right have you got to talk about him?

ERROL: As much right as you'll ever have. He'd have done
something about it.

ALVIN: About what?

ERROL: About everything! He wouldn't have turned into
some baldhead, weak-kneed, pink-arse, talking down to
his own black people and crying for sympathy when he
can't get no fucking answers.

ALVIN: You don't know.

ERROL: Oh, I fucking know alright 'cos he's my dad too, not
just yours. *(Picks up a picture of his mother off the top of the
cabinet and smashes it down.)* This is all you're fucking worth
now, white boy.

ALVIN: Stop it!

ERROL: Why don't you get your pink-arse out to work and
join her or go phone the bank and warn them that you
know of a black nigger who's bad and gonna pull a job?
My dad would have kicked your fuckin' head in! He'd
have swept aside all this shit and got to the heart of the
matter. Fear! You're shit-scared now!

*(He sweeps all the pictures off the cabinet top, pulls the mirror down
off the wall, and begins to stamp on it.)*

ALVIN: You mad bastard, stop it! Stop it!

*(They fight. Eventually ERROL knocks ALVIN out. He hits his head
as he falls. ERROL picks up his box and things and slowly makes*

his way out. He is bruised and dazed. As he shuts the door ALVIN
begins to stir. He is going to be alright.)

(The lights come down.)

END OF ACT TWO

Act Three

SCENE ONE

Lights up. Tuesday evening. We see ALVIN lying on the settee, holding a pack of ice to his eye which is blackened. The damaged pictures are back on top of the cabinet, and the mirror lies discarded in one corner. He is thinking uncomfortable thoughts.

We hear the door open and slam. MOTHER enters. At first she doesn't notice ALVIN then she sees his feet.

MOTHER: Alvin? *(She moves around.)* Alvin, what's happened? What's the matter with you?

ALVIN: Nothing, I'm alright.

MOTHER: What's the matter? What happened? Don't tell me nothing. I'm not blind.

ALVIN: I had an argument with Errol.

MOTHER: An argument?

ALVIN: A fight.

MOTHER: About what?

ALVIN: Nothing. I asked for it, I suppose. I'll be alright. It's just a bruise.

MOTHER: What the hell were you fighting over?

ALVIN: Nothing, I said. Let's just forget it.

MOTHER: I can't just forget it like that. Where is he?

ALVIN: I don't know. Down the club, I suppose. I didn't ask.

(MOTHER puts down her bag and takes off her coat.)

MOTHER: *(Unwinding a little.)* When did you get back?

ALVIN: A couple of hours ago.

MOTHER: That was quick.

ALVIN: What was?

MOTHER: The flight.

ALVIN: The flight was on time. I got a lift from the airport.

MOTHER: Who from?

ALVIN: Just someone I met on the plane, that's all. *(Sits up.)*
Why, didn't you want to see me?

MOTHER: Don't be silly. Of course I want to see you, it's just that
I thought I'd be back before you got here. I left something for
you in the oven in case I wasn't. Did you get it?

ALVIN: Yeah, Errol gave it to me. *(Gets up.)* Do you want a
cup of coffee or something?

MOTHER: I'll get it.

(She goes through into the kitchen and he sits down again.)

How was home, then? *(No answer.)* Well, how was it?

ALVIN: The worst two weeks of my life.

(Long pause. MOTHER comes back through with her drink.)

MOTHER: Errol was…

ALVIN: I don't want to talk about Errol. I've said all I've got
to say to him.

MOTHER: Well, I thought he'd be glad to have you back.
I'm glad to have you back. Can I give you a hug?
I suppose you think you're too old to kiss your mother
now… *(She hugs him but gets no response.)*

What's the matter? Is there something you want to tell me?

ALVIN: Was it a joke?

MOTHER: Was what a joke?

ALVIN: Sending me out there?

MOTHER: But you said you wanted to go.

ALVIN: Did I?

MOTHER: Alvin, when the telegram came…

ALVIN: When the telegram came you looked at it for an hour then opened it and told us that your dad was dead. Told us our grandfather, who neither of us can remember anyway, was dead. Then you went to get a cup of coffee, mumbling something about time off work being hard to get, and by the time you came back through with the three cups of coffee you'd had an idea. Why didn't I represent the three of us at the funeral? Give me a chance to see the island. Course I wanted to go!

MOTHER: But…

ALVIN: But under the circumstances, mother, I think you should have done your own dirty work.

MOTHER: What happened?

ALVIN: Oh, so you were expecting something to happen?

MOTHER: No I just want to know what all this is about. I sent you out there to my father's funeral because…

ALVIN: Yes, we know. Because you couldn't afford time off from work. I suppose all my life I've wanted to go back. All I really remembered about the island was leaving it and getting on a big dirty boat, full of scruffy, dirty people, as a confused kid of five. All that pushing and shouting. Historically I suppose it was a kind of second diaspora but all I knew was that my world was turning upside down and I clung tightly to your hand not knowing what the hell was going on. *(Pause.)* You know, for the last nineteen years I've wondered about that island, mother, about the people on it, what they're doing, who they are, and why I'm not back there with them, sitting in the sun and living the simple life of existence, with no worries and all that. I've wondered what I'd have been like if I'd stayed there, what I'd have done, and then it kept dawning on me that l shouldn't really be wondering at all. You should be telling me. You know, filling in the blanks 'cos the most important part of knowing where you're going to is knowing where you've come from, right? *(Pause.)* I guess till I was eighteen and went to university it was pretty easy. I worried but it was a kind of part-time worry 'cos my schoolwork was something I could channel all that energy and panic into. Try and prove something, I guess. An island unto myself and all that. But all that changed at university, especially in the last year where you've suddenly got to face the sick reality that your life's about to take a turn which'll nine times out of ten put you on the road you'll have to follow forever. Now what was I, a black boy who came from an island three thousand miles away, doing in the posh white university? Mother, what the hell did that dirty, scruffy, stinking boat have to do with all that lecturing and books, all that wealth and bloody ceremony? You've never talked to us. None of you do. To leave that place and get a 'proper job' or start a bloody career wasn't gonna give us any answers, it wasn't gonna give me any answers, it would probably just negate any chance of me ever finding them, so I decided to drop out, to hover in mid-air, and for the last two and a half years I've just waited and waited. Plenty of hollow rhetoric, plenty of passionate intensity, but still no answers. And then my grandfather died and you suggested I went 'home' and I thought yes, 'home', and yes, this is Babylon and yes, yes, yes I've got to go to my people and yes, I should have just got a job, any job, and saved and gone a long time ago, and yes, when I get back I want to take off for Africa so yes, I'll have to make plans to have some bread available to depart soon after I get back and we take over the leadership and yes, Errol was coming too. Answers. At last it was all happening, mother. The oscillation and the vacancy seemed to be coming to an end. First the West Indies then plunge into the deep end and visit the mother country – Africa. I bought a notebook in which I was going to keep notes for a book I was going to write about my two weeks in the West Indies and my trip to Africa. *Out of Exile: Free at Last* by Alvin Marshall. My first bestseller. Well go on then, laugh.

MOTHER: I'm not laughing, Alvin. Go on. What happened, please?

ALVIN: 'What happened, please!'

MOTHER: Alvin.

ALVIN: You know what they call you, mother? That is if they can be bothered to think of you in the first place. 'Miss Chalkie'. That's about as big an insult as they can think of. They daren't call you anything obscene, not that they don't want to, in case someone finds it funny. That's a measure of their hatred for you. They don't even laugh about you. After all this time you're not even a joke. I don't know why they bothered to send you the telegram. They knew you wouldn't come. I think they just wanted to make you feel guilty.

MOTHER: Alvin, listen to me…

ALVIN: No! You listen to me. Let me say what I've got to say, please. Your sister, Vera, met me at the airport. She was about the only one who talked to me the whole time I was there. She took me back to the house where I met your mother and brother too. It was getting late so the four of

us sat down for a meal and we were getting on fine, or so
I thought, until I told them how sorry you were that you
hadn't been able to make it for the funeral. 'Oh,' said Vera.
Your mother started to cry so your brother took her into
the other room. They didn't come out till I'd gone to bed.
The next day I went for a walk with Vera and she asked
after you and Errol, and Vernice and Charmain. So I told
her how things were and how they were in England and
what we were trying to do. She didn't give a damn really,
so I spent the next few days on my own, taking pictures,
talking to nobody, buying my own food in cafes, and just
coming back there to sleep. It was obvious they didn't
really want me there. Then the day of the funeral came.
I didn't have a suit so your brother lent me one and I
went. When we came back he asked for his suit, told me
to get out, and to tell you not to bother ever coming back.
It was as simple as that. I'd come for the funeral, it was
over now so I had to go. Oh, I nearly forgot. He told me
to tell you that your mother never wants to see you again.
I tried to tell him I had two more days before the plane
I was booked on left, but he just laughed. So I spent the
last two days in a rooming house with no money spare to
buy food. Time to do plenty of thinking and writing in, I
thought. Well, I certainly did a lot of thinking, but here…
(He gets up and goes across to his bags.) …let me show you
the notes I made for my first bestseller; that first classic of
decolonisation. See, nothing. Absolutely nothing. Not only
had my family treated me like a leper, but the island itself
was just riddled with corruption. Smuggling at customs
was so open and institutionalised, I couldn't believe it.
I was too ashamed of my own people to write down what
I found. *(Pause.)* Well, haven't you got anything to say,
mother? You know full well what you were sending me
out there for, so why didn't you tell me you were persona
non grata; that we all are. You know what they think of us?
They think we're cowards. White cowards.

MOTHER: Let them think what they want.

ALVIN: Do what, mother? You'll have to do a little better than that this time.

MOTHER: Listen to me, son.

ALVIN: Mother, I was born out of wedlock, right? Well? Okay, I'm a bastard. Where's my father's grave? Where's his cricket gear on display? I sat in that rooming house for two days, frightened sick to go to the Town Hall and look up the answers in the records there. I was frightened of what I might find. Well? Okay then, don't look so surprised.

MOTHER: I meant to tell you.

ALVIN: Like hell!

MOTHER: I wanted to tell you but I thought it might upset you.

ALVIN: Upset me?

MOTHER: I don't want to hurt any of you with this kind of thing. It's not important is it?

ALVIN: I wouldn't have cared less about being told I was a bastard, that's how much it would have upset me!

MOTHER: But I wasn't to know that.

ALVIN: Where's my father's grave? Where's this display of his cricket gear?

MOTHER: Didn't anyone tell you?

ALVIN: Why the hell should anyone tell me? Why the hell should I have to ask? Where! Where! Where!

MOTHER: I don't know.

ALVIN: What's that supposed to mean?

MOTHER: I mean, Alvin, that I've never seen your father's grave. He didn't die of cancer before we left. *(Pause.)* He was alive. He died only about two years ago. Vera wrote and told me about it.

ALVIN: You mean he's been alive all these years you've been telling us he was dead, and you knew about it?

MOTHER: You've got to understand, Alvin, that I couldn't tell you about it.

ALVIN: What do you mean you couldn't? You mean you wouldn't. You...you...

MOTHER: He was no good for you all. That's why we left him behind and escaped to England.

ALVIN: What do you mean, escaped? What was he, a mass fucking murderer or something?

MOTHER: Your father was a cricketer, like I've always told you, but he took to drink and I didn't want my children brought up in a house with a drunk. Sometimes he'd disappear for days, and then come in in the middle of the night and smash up the furniture in his drunken rage. He'd wake you all up with the noise, take whatever money I had, and that would be the last we'd see of him for a few more days. What the hell did you want me to do? Let it go on until one day he turned on one of us and killed us? It was a living hell, Alvin. I couldn't cope with you all and him and anyhow, what kind of an education did you think you were all going to get on that island? What kind of life were we going to be able to lead with him acting like an animal? What kind of life was I going to have?

ALVIN: What did you do to him?

MOTHER: What did I do to him?

ALVIN: What did you do to him? Cricketers don't just suddenly go mad overnight for no reason. Gary Sobers didn't go out and knock up two hundred one day, and come out to bowl in a straitjacket and foaming at the mouth the next. *(Pause.)* Or was he mad when you eventually decided to make it legal?

MOTHER: Alvin!

ALVIN: Well, come on. Was he mad when you married him, or did you drive him round the bloody bend?

MOTHER: No.

ALVIN: Well, what did you do to him, then? What did you do to drive my father mad and leave him to an unmarked grave?

MOTHER: Nothing. It was him.

ALVIN: Well, I'm waiting.

MOTHER: When he was picked for the team for the second time.

ALVIN: The West Indies?

MOTHER: Yes.

ALVIN: Well?

MOTHER: Well, he tried to organise a boycott and come out on strike. He wanted the team to refuse to play.

ALVIN: Why?

MOTHER: Because, Alvin, you've got to understand that up until then the captain of the West Indies had always been white and your father felt it ought to be a black man. He wanted to be captain himself, and everyone said he ought to be the captain. He was, Alvin, the best all-rounder the island had ever seen. Wallace Marshall. He could do it all, son.

ALVIN: And what happened?

MOTHER: Nobody signed their contracts and it looked
like the tour was off unless Wallace was made captain
but... But, someone from London flew out and offered
everybody except Wallace twice the money, plus bonuses,
to sign up.

ALVIN: And?

MOTHER: And? They signed of course. Three days later the
team took off on the tour without your father.

ALVIN: Still with a white captain?

MOTHER: Your father's life collapsed, Alvin. He lived for
cricket. He knew nothing else, so what else could he do?
He started to drink. Errol was only a few months old at
the time, and at first I managed to hide it from my parents.
But then he came round one time in a drunken rage when
Vernice and Wilfred were visiting. They felt they ought to
get Wallace some help so they told my mother, who came
to live with us, and my father offered to look after Wallace.
He wouldn't have it. He said he wanted us, his family,
and my mother left. The day she left us and Wallace came
back was the last time I saw her, but it was no good.
I didn't want to live with a drunk, I didn't want you all
to...to... *(She begins to cry.)*

ALVIN: Mother...

MOTHER: No, I want to go on. You said you wanted to hear.
What the hell was I supposed to do, then? Hope you all
wouldn't notice, that it would all go away like magic? Well,
it wasn't going away, Alvin. It was getting worse. I had to
get out. We had to get out. So we came to England.

ALVIN: We ran away to England.

MOTHER: We had to, Alvin.

ALVIN: Why didn't you tell us all this before instead of just pretending.

MOTHER: I didn't want you to make him into an idol of some kind, a hero.

ALVIN: Well, what's all this about a display of his cricket gear, then? And what's all this about telling us how good he was... What's that if not making a hero out of him?

MOTHER: But I wanted you to be proud of him. You should be proud of him, but not follow him. You've both got an education and advantages that he never had and I've worked myself stupid to get you where you are now. You can stand up on your own two feet and rise up out of the gutter. I just don't understand why you all want to wallow in the filth and...

ALVIN: Is that what you think of Vernice, then? The gutter. Wallowing in filth with no education, no certificates.

MOTHER: No, of course not...

ALVIN: But we're better? My father probably died a tramp and a broken man. A drunk. Vernice's husband died an electrician. He died in his sleep in the warmth of his English bed. I can live with what my father was. I could have lived with it before, but don't you think Errol has a right to know about him now?

MOTHER: Errol has problems of his own.

ALVIN: And you're the cause of most of them.

MOTHER: Not this one.

ALVIN: What one?

MOTHER: Shelley's pregnant.

ALVIN: What?

MOTHER: I didn't go to school today. I hardly slept for a moment last night worrying. I went and met Shelley as she was going to collect the results of her pregnancy test. Errol's going to be a father.

ALVIN: And does Errol know?

MOTHER: He may do by now. Shelley's gone to meet him at the club.

ALVIN: Jesus Christ! Did he know she thought she was pregnant?

MOTHER: No. Shelley didn't want to tell him till she was sure.

ALVIN: I don't believe it.

MOTHER: She said he was always in the wrong mood.

ALVIN: And of course you weren't going to tell your own son that he was well on the way to becoming a father.

MOTHER: I only found out yesterday.

ALVIN: If you can't tell your own son that he may be about to become a father then something is very wrong. You know, I just don't believe it! I thought I had it all worked out and everything. You know what I was gonna do, mother? Social work. I thought, if I'm gonna stay here I might as well contribute. This place, Britain, is full of shit, but where else is there? But mother! I can't stay here with you. Every time you open your mouth another pillar tumbles. One of us has to go. It's as simple as that. Either you leave me alone or I... I don't know. Leave us both alone.

MOTHER: What do you mean, Alvin?

ALVIN: I'll tell you what I mean. Remember the 1968 Olympics and the John Carlos, Tommie Smith, Black Power thing, the salute; and I said to you in joy, how all the black people were winning for once, and how I was over the moon about it...and you hit me. And when

I wanted to do a project on sugar 'cos I knew it came from the West Indies and you told me real sugar grew in England and you said I had to do it on sugar beet. Okay. And when I told you the reason you're still on the bottom scale of teaching even though you're the highest qualified and longest serving you shouted at me and then wouldn't talk to me for days. Now is it just this bastard country or is it the two of you in partnership that are dragging us under? Good God, I go half way round the world and back thinking I'd made some sort of discovery and come back to find the same damn lies, the same white lies, the same black lies. The same shame; the same fear; the same shallowness. You're no better than Errol. You're different sides of the same coin, but you're worse if anything 'cos you've got the whole truth to play with and you still distort it. You haven't even got the decency to afford either of us that luxury. Why? Why?

MOTHER: For you! For you all! You two are all I've got. Everything I've ever done has been for the two of you, Alvin. Please leave me alone now. Can't you see that I did it all for you?

ALVIN: Leave you alone? You who presides up above, determining our destinies, keeping the answers to yourself yet asking all the questions.

MOTHER: Stop it! Stop it!

ALVIN: Do you want to see us two end up in unmarked graves, eh? Do you want to see Errol with a bottle in one hand, banging his head against a brick wall like our dad? You spend all day helping someone else's child…

MOTHER: What do you want me to do? Let her walk the streets? Her parents are putting her out and do you want me to let her panic and suffer because of my son?

ALVIN: Your son! He's no more your son than bloody
    Winston Churchill's your son. There's no point of contact.
    Oh, I'm sure you want to help Shelley through. After
    all, you can see her problem. It's material! It's physical.
    It's going to be born soon, but when it's black, when it's
    in the mind, you just run. You run as you ran from our
    dad and your family, and for years you've been running
    away from us. Did you think that going down to Ram
    Jams was a passing phase like a pop group or platform
    soles? Do you think that we don't want to be happy and
    have some money and live like everyone else? Do you
    think it's all just a big joke, or can't any of you see any
    further than your precious white respectability and your
    bastard mortgages? You've blown it this time, haven't
    you? It's your game, your rules. Well? Can't you see we
    need protecting? There's enough black people in lunatic
    asylums as it is. *(He gets up to move away.)*

MOTHER: Where are you going?

ALVIN: That's it? That's it exactly! Instead of saying 'don't
    go'! It's here! The facts in my opinion are this and I
    think you ought to consider that. It's just 'where are
    you going?' – 'you're wasting your life' – 'get a proper
    job' – 'dress smartly' – 'do up your tie' – clichés for the
    white boy! Well? Well no! I demand more than being told
    that I'm not in the gutter and that I'm to dress properly.
    I want to know why I'm black. I want to know all that
    you know about being black. I want to know what
    blackness has meant to you – to your father, or your
    father's father's father. I want to know how to defend
    myself. I want to know how you've defended yourself,
    how my father coped, how we all have got this far, and
    sadly only you can give me the answers, but you refuse. I
    don't want no Africa or Caribbean anymore; I don't want
    to compromise. I want answers, 'cos I'm going under,
    and if I'm not going to get any answers then I need help

but the only people who can help me are either too busy playing white or too busy playing black, understand! Understand!

MOTHER: Alvin!

ALVIN: I don't need your lies anymore. Not now, not ever. I've told you, it's me or you.

MOTHER: What do you want, Alvin?

ALVIN: Right now I want some ice for my eye.

(He goes into the kitchen to get some silence. We hear the back door open and shut.)

VERNICE: Is she back yet?

ALVIN: Through there.

VERNICE: What happen?

ALVIN: Nothing.

(VERNICE comes through. ALVIN slides the door shut behind her.)

VERNICE: What happen to Alvin?

MOTHER: He hurt his eye fighting with Errol.

VERNICE: Lord, me thought the pair uh them come too ol' for that sorta thing. What happen?

MOTHER: For Christ's sake, I don't want to talk about it, Vernice.

VERNICE: Girl, me tired like hell too, so don't bite off me head, huh.

MOTHER: I'm sorry.

VERNICE: Well, I tell you, you shoulda tell the boy. You can't say me ain't warn you. At least me try. Anyway, Stanley ask me to marry him again. Vivien?

MOTHER: I'm listening.

VERNICE: But...

MOTHER: But what?

VERNICE: Charmain leaving.

MOTHER: Leaving what?

VERNICE: Leaving home, leaving me because she say she hate Stanley, because she say she goin' hate me if I marry him.

MOTHER: Well, I don't know what to say.

VERNICE: *(Quietly.)* At least she talking to me again.

MOTHER: What are you going to do?

VERNICE: What can I do? I thought you might talk to her and explain.

MOTHER: Explain what, Vernice?

VERNICE: Explain that Stanley is a fine man, or mebbe you ain't think so?

MOTHER: Of course I do.

VERNICE: Do you know what the last eight years have been like for me without Wilfred, girl? The first few years me down the club so every night an' me doing it so often I think uh starting to charge, but Charmain too small to know about that. And then when she start to come bigger I try an' settle down with a man. You remember Charlie? Then Rudy? No-good bastards. Only Stanley's been any good to me, given me money an' love. Remember love?

MOTHER: I remember love.

VERNICE: Can't you talk to her?

MOTHER: It's blood they want, Vernice, not talking to.

VERNICE: Vivien, listen to me, girl. Me can't remember the last time I say please to you or anybody else, but can't you help me out please?

MOTHER: Vernice.

VERNICE: Can't you ask Alvin, then. Can't he come an' talk to she.

MOTHER: Alvin?

VERNICE: Why not? Me ain't thinka nobody else she goin' listen to.

(ALVIN opens the door and comes through. He has discarded the ice pack.)

ALVIN: What? Well you called me.

(He picks up his jacket.)

MOTHER: I wasn't calling you.

VERNICE: It was me. I wonder if you could come across an' talk to Charmain. She say she upset an' want to leave home.

ALVIN: What's the matter with her, then? Well? Why's she so upset?

VERNICE: I don't know but...

ALVIN: Well, when you find out let me know. I'm off for a walk round the block to get some fresh air.

MOTHER: Alvin.

ALVIN: Don't worry. I said I'm just going for a walk. I'll be back. I'm not gonna throw myself under a bus or anything. *(He goes.)*

VERNICE: Girl, don't look so. He ain't goin' do nothing stupid.

MOTHER: How do you know?

VERNICE: I don't. Me jus' trying to help. If you want make an enemy outa me now, well jus' go ahead an' do it for me think that be what you want.

MOTHER: Vernice, that's not what I want, and you know it. I just want my kids back, that's all. I just want for us both to be happy again.

VERNICE: Happy! Like when the hell the last time we both happy together? I mean the botha us really happy? Never in England. No.

(MOTHER begins to cry.)

Jesus girl, pull you all self together. People ain't take no notice uh tears anymore. They gone outa fashion an' there ain't much we can do about it.

MOTHER: Sorry.

VERNICE: But nothing to be sorry about. As for meself, well, I suppose me gotta make a choice.

MOTHER: No you haven't.

VERNICE: No choice?

MOTHER: No choice.

VERNICE: Sharp as ever.

MOTHER: Wish I was.

VERNICE: Did you go to work today?

MOTHER: No.

VERNICE: I'm glad.

(They hug each other.)

111

I'll go telephone him and tell him it's just two pints a day and no cream from now on.

MOTHER: Wait! There's somebody at the door. I don't want to be alone if it's Errol.

VERNICE: Why? You had a bust-up with him too?

(Enter ERROL and SHELLEY from the hall. SHELLEY is carrying a suitcase.)

SHELLEY: Hello, Miss.

VERNICE: Boy, I hope you ain't come back here to cause you all mother no more trouble, for she got enough on she plate as it is.

ERROL: I ain't come back here to cause nobody any trouble, and I ain't come back to listen to you or anybody else, so why don't you just get off my back. When I wanna be insulted ask somebody black to do it. *(He moves to go upstairs.)*

SHELLEY: Shall… Shall I wait here, Errol?

ERROL: Wait there. *(Without turning to look at her he goes upstairs.)*

MOTHER: You better go and ring Stanley. I'll be alright now.

VERNICE: Girl, me ain't want to leave you if you is still so.

MOTHER: There's nothing to worry about, Vernice. I'll call round to see the pair of you later.

VERNICE: Girl, things looking better already. *(To SHELLEY.)* Don't let him bully you so. Tell him where to get off, you hear me?

SHELLEY: *(Nervously.)* Yes.

(VERNICE goes via the kitchen.)

MOTHER: Well?

SHELLEY: I waited for him by the club, Miss and…

MOTHER: And?

SHELLEY: And eventually he came down. I think he's fallen out with Alvin.

MOTHER: Go on.

SHELLEY: He told me to get lost, Miss, and then I told him, 'cos I thought he was going to hit me, but I didn't tell him that you knew or anything. I just said that I was having his baby and he laughed. He wasn't angry with me or anything, Miss, he just laughed, and then he kissed me and said we were going away.

MOTHER: Going away where?

SHELLEY: Africa, I think. He said we were going to have a warrior.

MOTHER: Oh my God!

SHELLEY: He said this warrior would come back and haunt you and everybody else. He said we'd have to get ready, for the time was near, so he sent me home to pack and get me things while he waited at the club for us. Me mum and dad were out for once and so I got everything and he's upstairs getting his stuff now.

MOTHER: You're going now?

SHELLEY: Yes, Miss. Tonight. Somewhere in Africa. Errol's going to get a job as an economic adviser to the freedom fighters.

MOTHER: What freedom fighters, Shelley?

SHELLEY: The African freedom fighters.

MOTHER: Africa? Tonight. For Christ's sake, Shelley, grow up.

SHELLEY: Miss?

MOTHER: What do you want, Shelley? I mean what do you really want more than anything else?

SHELLEY: Miss, I've never had nothing. It's easy for you but I love Errol and I want to have our baby. I might never get a second chance. Me mum and dad hate each other and since me dad got laid off at the factory last year it's just got worse. All he does is just stay in bed then go down the betting shop or the boozer and the only excitement he gets is telling me what a slut I am and hitting me mum. And she can't leave him 'cos she hasn't got anywhere else to go, Miss. She's older than him and in five or six years she'll be on her pension. You wouldn't think she was my mum if you saw her. When I said I wanted to stay on at school they said they'd kick me out. I told you that, Miss. I've got to fend for meself now.

MOTHER: Safety of a family? Protection?

SHELLEY: Suppose so, Miss. He'll have to love his baby at least.

MOTHER: And you love him?

SHELLEY: Yes, Miss.

MOTHER: You love him enough to leave schoolwork and your family? You love him enough to believe that he'll give you what you want, Shelley? 'Top of the Pops' security.

SHELLEY: Yes, Miss. We're having a baby, Miss.

MOTHER: You're so young.

SHELLEY: Everybody says that, but I don't feel it. I can look after meself.

MOTHER: Can you? Can you look after yourself and Errol? Can you look after yourself and Errol and the baby, Shelley?

SHELLEY: I won't have to Miss, cos there'll be Errol.

MOTHER: But Shelley, you're so sure.

SHELLEY: I've got to be, Miss, or I couldn't do it. I'm old enough to think for meself now.

MOTHER: You do realise that if you all give up, my children stand no chance.

SHELLEY: Miss?

MOTHER: Nothing, Shelley. Look, the African freedom fighters.

SHELLEY: Yes, Miss.

MOTHER: How are you going to get to Africa, Shelley?

SHELLEY: Errol's taking care of that.

MOTHER: He is, is he?

SHELLEY: Yes, Miss.

MOTHER: *(Goes for her handbag.)* Take this key, Shelley, and I want you to use it if you have to. It's the key to the front door.

SHELLEY: But Miss, Errol's got one.

MOTHER: Errol mustn't know that you've got one as well. My house is your house now, and I want you to remember that. If you don't want to go back to your parents, if things go wrong, then you don't have to, understand? I want you to take it.

SHELLEY: *(Takes the key.)* Okay. I'll be fine, Miss, but thanks anyway.

MOTHER: Promise you won't lose it.

SHELLEY: I won't lose it, Miss. Thanks.

(We hear a shot go off upstairs. SHELLEY screams.)

MOTHER: Oh my God!

(She restrains SHELLEY.)

SHELLEY: Errol? Errol!

MOTHER: Oh my God, no!

SHELLEY: Let me go, Miss. Let me go!

MOTHER: No! I'll go. I'm going. Stay here.

SHELLEY: *(Clawing at MOTHER.)* But, Miss. Let me go!

MOTHER: Shelley, stop it. Get off, Shelley. Leave me alone!

SHELLEY: Errol! Errol!

(MOTHER tries to break free and get upstairs. The front door crashes open and ALVIN comes in.)

ALVIN: What's happened?

(He doesn't wait for an answer. He rushes upstairs.)

MOTHER: *(Stays put.)* Oh my God, Errol.

SHELLEY: *(In tears.)* Miss, I love him.

(VERNICE rushes in.)

VERNICE: What was that? What's goin' on? Vivien?

SHELLEY: Errol's shot himself.

VERNICE: Oh my God! Is Alvin up there?

(SHELLEY nods.)

Jesus Christ! Ain't nobody goin' phone for the ambulance
or the police or what?

(She goes across to the phone and begins to dial. ALVIN comes down.)

ALVIN: Leave it.

VERNICE: But…

ALVIN: I said leave it. We don't need it.

(SHELLEY screams and MOTHER looks like she's going to faint.)

VERNICE: *(Runs to MOTHER.)* God have mercy on his soul.

ALVIN: He's alright.

SHELLEY: *(Goes towards the steps.)* Errol!

ALVIN: *(Holds her back.)* I said he's alright. He's coming down.

SHELLEY: Errol!

(Enter ERROL, with a suitcase and the brown parcel, which clearly contains the weapons. SHELLEY moves towards him but he stops her with his gaze.)

Are you okay, Errol?

ERROL: Course I'm okay. Just look at you all. A real picture of fucking concern. Don't worry. *(He gestures to the parcel.)* I'm taking them with me.

VERNICE: Boy, you sick.

ERROL: I'm sick? Me? Just take a look at yourselves.

VERNICE: Don't talk to you all mother so. Leave it for you stinking friends and that she there beside you, but you leave you mother outa this, you hear me?

ERROL: She is carrying my child. My baby. Surprised? Didn't think I knew what I was doing? You all didn't think I could hold the pressure, but we're all dead men talking to dead men but futility is no theory. It's not reality or brutality. My child shall live. It's a sign.

VERNICE: What is a sign?

ERROL: A child; my child.

VERNICE: You'd better ask she about that.

ERROL: It's either mine or it's an immaculate conception!
A leader is born in the promised land.

VERNICE: Me better phone a doctor.

ALVIN: No.

MOTHER: *(Weakly.)* Errol, listen to me.

ERROL: Listen to you, mother? What, again? Listen to you
some more, mother?

MOTHER: I want to talk with you. We all do.

ERROL: Oh, do we all?

MOTHER: Alvin and I...

ERROL: Oh, come now. Let's leave Snow White out of this.

VERNICE: You want to look to you woman, boy.

ERROL: Don't 'boy' me, woman. I don't give a fuck about her
and she knows it.

MOTHER: Please listen, Errol.

ERROL: Go tell it to the white man but don't come tainting
my black ears.

VERNICE: You nasty-minded little bastard.

ERROL: I think you've got the wrong one there.

ALVIN: Get out, Errol.

ERROL: Talking to me, nigger?

ALVIN: I said just go, for God's sake.

ERROL: You want me to black up your other eye, white boy?

ALVIN: For Christ's sake if you're going, then go, but leave her alone now.

ERROL: What, so you can comfort your mummy, Social Worker?

ALVIN: I've got no more comfort for her than I have for you, so just go.

ERROL: Don't you want to know where I'm going?

ALVIN: No.

ERROL: *(Pulls out five hundred pounds.)* Shelley's been peddling her arse. Doing a bit of whoring on the side for me.

SHELLEY: That's not true!

ALVIN: You bastard!

ERROL: *(Pulls out a knife.)* Another step, nigger, and I'll cut you so bad boy.

MOTHER: Shelley.

SHELLEY: It's my money, Miss, but I didn't.

VERNICE: You didn't what? Get your arse out of the house an' take him with you.

(ERROL picks up his suitcase and moves out towards the door.)

ERROL: I'm off to Africa. You're the ones that need a fucking doctor, not me.

(He goes towards the front door. SHELLEY picks up her case and follows him. She has no choice.)

VERNICE: The boy's sick.

MOTHER: Alvin, can't you stop him?

ALVIN: Stop him? Me stop him and you didn't even open your own mouth to stop him. He's gone out of that door as ignorant as he came in, and even after you've told me what you have, I'm still as ignorant as I was before. I don't understand what you're playing at. Stop him? I'm in no position to stop me, let alone him. Words can't stop him now. Words can't help.

VERNICE: You both want you all damn heads examining.

ALVIN: Listen, you better put your own house in order. You aren't exactly a paragon of virtue yourself.

VERNICE: I have done put me house in order an' I won't be makin' the same mistake again.

ALVIN: Well, think yourself lucky that you got to it before the dam broke 'cos some of us ain't so fucking fortunate.

(He storms upstairs.)

VERNICE: Are you alright, Vivien?

MOTHER: Alright? Alright! When my son's just left home after calling me everything under the sun. Every dirty, filthy name he could think of. Am I alright?

VERNICE: I sorry, girl. Why you not come and sit down, nuh? *(They go across and sit.)* What the boy doing with guns, anyhow?

MOTHER: Vernice, how the hell am I supposed to know! I'm just their mother, for God's sake! I just work my damn fingers to the bone for twenty-five and odd years, doing everything from typist to teacher so they have two crusts of bread on their plate and clothes on their backs. I just take them to a country halfway round the world, where they can live and grow up, I just turn my back on my own family for them, I just love once, just once, for them. Vernice, I'm just their mother. Nearly fifty. Old. Tired.

Lonely. What am I supposed to do? Why should I be told that my son has his bedroom full of guns and God knows what else? Why should I know? Who am I to be talked to? To be told?

VERNICE: Okay, girl. Okay.

MOTHER: It's not okay, it's not! I'm sick of being ignored and pushed around by them; being looked down on. I've got my pride. I've done my fair share of suffering too. I'm sick to death of being criticised by them both. I'm sick! Sick! What the hell do they want?

VERNICE: I don't know.

MOTHER: Well, I'm damned if I do. You know, I just don't care anymore. For the first time in my life I've had it. Up to here. There's just nothing left anyone can do to me anymore. Nothing.

(ALVIN comes downstairs with his flight bag and suitcase.)

VERNICE: Where you going?

ALVIN: I think you've said enough. *(To MOTHER.)* I'm going now.

MOTHER: Going?

ALVIN: Yes, going.

MOTHER: Going where? You've only just come back.

ALVIN: I don't know, mother. I said it was me or you. One of us had to go and I meant it. You didn't tell me, you didn't tell him, I can't live here, I can't live there. What am I supposed to do? What we supposed to do? Live on a raft in the middle of the Atlantic at a point equidistant between Africa, the Caribbean and Britain? Is that what you want us to do? Leave us till we sink? Till there's no trace of us? Lost between two waves, yet another black generation is dispossessed.

MOTHER: What are you talking about? Dispossessed from what?

ALVIN: I've spent the last few hours trying to get some kind of truth into Errol and some kind of truth out of you. I've been stretched tight like a piece of elastic between you both and I haven't a clue which one of you is right. All I know is that I can't be right 'cos I don't know what I'm talking about. Even now as I talk how do I know I'm not talking crap? Things are changing too quickly and all three of us tearing each other to pieces, conflict, conflict, conflict! Everywhere people playing at being something they aren't, everywhere someone so sure, so convinced that they've just got to be wrong. What the hell is going on? You don't know, right? Well, neither do I. The longer I stay here the more strain there's going to be and eventually I'll snap. I'll flip out and end up like Errol.

MOTHER: What do you mean end up like Errol?

ALVIN: Where do you think he's going? Africa? We might as well start digging his grave now.

MOTHER: Alvin!

ALVIN: Listen. He hasn't even got a passport.

MOTHER: But he applied for one. He has a passport.

ALVIN: Mother, mother, mother. When they asked him his nationality he put down... He put down African. And place of birth? The Dark Continent. They must have died laughing in the passport office.

MOTHER: Well, what's he going to do?

ALVIN: Errol's twenty-one and he can swim, after a fashion, for a while at least. Then, unless something happens, he'll sink.

MOTHER: Alvin! He's your brother!

ALVIN: And my dad was your husband! I've said all I've got to say.

MOTHER: Alvin! For Christ's sake, I've done my best. What do you want? What is it you all want from me?

ALVIN: From you, mother, nothing. You've got nothing left to give me. None of you have.

MOTHER: But you're all I've got. You're all I've lived for...

ALVIN: Sorry, mother.

(He turns and goes via the front doorway.)

MOTHER: Alvin! I'll do anything for you all, you know that. Alvin? Alvin!

(She cries.)

VERNICE: It's no use, girl. He's gone. They've both gone.

MOTHER: Oh my God!

VERNICE: They'll be back, don't worry.

MOTHER: No they won't. They won't be back. Oh my God!

VERNICE: They will. Vivien. Stop it. Tears ain't goin' help. I tell you that before. Why you not come over an' sit with me, nuh?

MOTHER: Jesus Lord Almighty, help me! Help me!

VERNICE: Come on now, girl. Come on. Calm down, nuh?

MOTHER: Vernice, leave me alone, please.

VERNICE: I don't think me should, girl.

MOTHER: Please leave me alone. I'll be alright now. Could you just please get me a glass of water and I'll be alright.

(VERNICE goes through and gets it.)

123

VERNICE: Look, girl, if me leave you I going come back in an hour. *(She comes back through.)* I have to make up Charmain's tea and give she some spending money then I goin' come back.

MOTHER: I'll be alright.

VERNICE: Sure?

MOTHER: Sure I'm sure.

VERNICE: Well. Gimme a smile, nuh. *(MOTHER gives her a faint smile.)* It goin' come alright. By tomorrow you done forget the whole thing an' everything goin' back to normal.

MOTHER: Alright.

VERNICE: I see you then, girl. I jus' go see to she.

MOTHER: Alright… Vernice?

VERNICE: What?

MOTHER: Thanks for everything. I don't know how I'd have managed without you.

VERNICE: *(Sucks teeth.)* Girl, you jus' start to learn at last. We got to stick together, nuh?

(She goes. MOTHER remains motionless for a few moments after the back door has shut. She looks across at Wallace's picture on the cabinet. She moves very slowly and with great dignity. She gets up and goes round to the drawer. She takes her glass of water with her. She takes out two bottles of pills, empties some into her hand and swallows them. She takes a drink. She repeats until both bottles are empty. She comes back round and sits on the settee, her body heaving with tears. She leans over the arm of the settee and doesn't move anymore.

We hear a key at the door. MOTHER doesn't respond. ALVIN comes in. He presumes her asleep. He puts down his bags and goes across to the cabinet where he takes the broken picture of her and looks at it. He comes across and stands over her. He can't say anything. He goes back and puts the picture in his bag and takes out the bottle of rum. He comes across and places it beside her. He kisses her on the top of the head. He can't see her face. He picks up his bag and goes.

Lights down.)

END OF PLAY

WHERE THERE IS DARKNESS

Characters

ALBERT WILLIAMS
RUTH WILLIAMS
MURIEL WILLIAMS
REMI WILLIAMS
SONJA JONES
HUSTON STEWART
VINCE
LYNN
NURSE

The play is set in the late 1970s and at various
points in the mid-1950s.

Act One

It is about ten p.m. A bright moonlit night. The lights come up on the back of a large detached house in one of London's residential commuter suburbs. A glass-panelled conservatory has been built out from the room and contains a basketchair and house plants, etc. A cool breeze plays with the long, full, rich curtains of the dining room. Upstairs the lights are off and the curtains are drawn. On the patio is a small, round, white metallic table with chairs to match. On the table top there are drinks and little bowls, trays and wooden leaves of peanuts, crisps, potato chips, etc., most of which are largely undisturbed. In front of the patio and down onto the forestage is the garden which is grassed and paved. There are trees in the garden. There are also silly little plastic gnomes. Draped from the trees, and extending back to the house, are fairy lights which in the dark give off a festive rainbow of colours. There are speakers both in the dining room and in the conservatory and we hear some classical music playing softly in the background. The actual hi-fi equipment is not in view. We can see that the dining room, though well and modernly furnished, has the odd cardboard box in sight, ready for final packing. There is a celebratory but uneasy feel to the set.

One can clearly hear the noise of a small party going on. The clinking of glasses blends with soft nervous laughter. Then ALBERT appears in the conservatory, having drifted out from the dining room. ALBERT is in his mid to late forties, going snowy on top and thinning out some. He is not a physically challenging man, though he is a little stocky. He wears a pair of flared crimplene trousers and a shortsleeved shirt of the same material. On his feet he has sandals and socks.

He holds his head as if he has a raging headache then slowly begins to walk down the garden. He seems to savour the feel of the grass and paving beneath his feet. RUTH appears in the conservatory behind him, holding a glass in her hand. She stands and looks at her husband. She is in her early thirties, white, dressed in a light, shoulderless evening dress. She is plain and obviously pleasant: a good companion.

RUTH: Albert?

ALBERT: *(Without turning around.)* So what happen, you can't see me?

RUTH: I've brought your drink for you.

ALBERT: You think someone might thief it if you leave it on the sideboard, is that it? You think England come so bad that a man can't put down a drink in his own house without someone thiefing it off?

RUTH: I just thought you might like it, that's all.

(Pause.)

Shall I let you know when Remi arrives?

ALBERT: *(Laughs.)* So you is butler now. You want me buy you a gong to bang and a silver tray to walk with?

(Pause.)

Remi has a tongue in his head. He can come out here himself and let me know when he arrives. I want to talk with the boy.

RUTH: I think I'd better see to the guests now. The Parry-Jones have just arrived.

ALBERT: Well you better go see to them or maybe is exit visa you're waiting for.

(RUTH goes back inside. Pause. ALBERT walks further down the garden. He talks to himself.) Remi can come out here, when he does arrive, and he can speak for himself.

HUSTON: *(Offstage.)* So you turn up to speak for yourself.

(Pause.)

Well sit down then nuh, boy. Sit down.

ALBERT: *(Sitting down in a confused manner.)* Sit down?

HUSTON: *(Offstage.)* Yes man, sit down. Sit!

ALBERT: *(Sitting.)* Thank you.

HUSTON: *(Offstage.)* You want a drink of water, take a drink.

ALBERT: Yes sir.

(He looks around but can't see a jug of water or a glass or anything.)

(HUSTON appears. Lighting change from the bright moonlight of the garden to the hard sunlight of the Caribbean, ALBERT takes out a large white handkerchief and mops his brow. HUSTON is in his early fifties. He is dressed in long trousers, open sandals, and a bright cotton short-sleeved shirt with a palm tree pattern. He has on dark glasses. He is carrying a glass of water.)

HUSTON: Well, you want one or not?

ALBERT: No thank you.

HUSTON: Well to me, Leeward Island breeze means a dozen jugs of water per day. Well, we have some talking to do, then?

ALBERT: Yes sir.

HUSTON: Well, come on then. I got a business to run out front and since me wife pass on I don't have nobody to help me deal with the customers.

ALBERT: Yes sir, I appreciate that.

HUSTON: Appreciate what? Me daughter should be here helping me out instead of waiting on your arse hand and foot.

ALBERT: It's Muriel I want to talk about.

HUSTON: What you done to she?

133

ALBERT: *(Quickly.)* Nothing...except...

HUSTON: Speak up.

ALBERT: I would like to ask your permission to marry she. To marry, Muriel, your daughter.

HUSTON: You don't have to tell me twice. I know who it is you talking about.

(Pause.)

When you decide this?

ALBERT: This week.

(Pause.)

HUSTON: You love she?

ALBERT: Yes sir.

HUSTON: Well, is a start, I suppose.

ALBERT: She means everything to me and...

HUSTON: Look boy, leave that shit for she. You don't have to sell the deal to me. This don't be business talk, is family talk, you understand.

(Under his breath.)

'She means everything to me and...'

(Pause.)

She want to marry you?

ALBERT: Yes sir.

HUSTON: And when you all planning on getting married?

ALBERT: Two weeks Sunday.

HUSTON: So soon?

ALBERT: Yes sir.

(Pause.)

HUSTON: Well, I suppose haste is no more of a sin than what you already been committing. Her mother would turn in she grave.

(He takes a drink, then turns on him sharply.)

Well, that's all then. I don't see no problems, but mark you, I want a proper invitation on a proper card.

ALBERT: Muriel's going to see to that tomorrow.

HUSTON: Yes, I bet she is.

(Pause.)

I going reply formally when I get the invitation but between the both of us I going be there lest the Lord decide to put me out me misery first.

ALBERT: Thank you.

(Pause. HUSTON has a final drink and puts down the glass.)

HUSTON: Well, you going or what?

ALBERT: Maybe I should tell you that Muriel is expecting a baby.

HUSTON: *(Calmly, almost sarcastically.)* Yes, maybe you should tell me that.

ALBERT: For the baby's sake. We thought we'd get married for its sake.

HUSTON: Boy, you got some nerve, don't you? Coming in here and telling me you going marry me daughter after you drag she out of the bosom of she family. And then

135

you sit there now and tell me you just put she with child, my grandchild, and you telling me it as a P.S., as an afterthought or something.

ALBERT: No sir…

HUSTON: Yes boy! Yes boy! Not 'no sir'. You can't control yourself or what? Answer me! You can't control yourself?

ALBERT: We…

HUSTON: I not talking about 'we', I talking about you!

(He stabs his finger right up to ALBERT's face.)

VOICE: *(Offstage: impatiently.)* Huston! Do I get any service around here or you want me take my trade somewhere else?

HUSTON: *(Hopping into his 'shop' voice.)* I'll be with you in just one moment, please.

(To ALBERT.)

When the child due?

ALBERT: Six months.

HUSTON: *(In an aggressive whisper, gesturing at him.)* She going get the best treatment is possible, you hear me? Tomorrow I want you to go hire the white nurse to supervise the pregnancy.

What is blasted well done is done. Is no use crying over spilt milk.

ALBERT: No sir.

HUSTON: You don't watch over she and I going break every bone in your body, you understand?

(ALBERT nods. HUSTON points hard.) Every bone in your frigging body.

(He goes off into the shop.)

(Offstage.)

Sorry to keep you waiting…

(ALBERT stands slowly. He holds his head in his hands and shakes it as if with disbelief.)

(The lights slowly begin to change back to the present and RUTH reappears again in the conservatory.)

RUTH: Can you wait just a second? He's in the garden – I'll go and fetch him.

(She comes out into the garden and walks down towards ALBERT.)

Albert, it's late now. The guests, they're ready to leave.

(He looks up and rubs some life back into his face.)

ALBERT: Is you Ruth? What you doing here?

RUTH: What?

ALBERT: I don't feel so good.

(Pause.)

They gone?

RUTH: They're waiting Albert – for you to see them out.

ALBERT: Waiting for me?

RUTH: Yes.

ALBERT: I see. So is me who come fucking butler now.

(He walks off into the house leaving RUTH behind. RUTH moves off to the table where she begins to pick nervously at the peanuts. She

licks the salt off a peanut and puts it back down in a little bowl. Offstage we hear voices.)

ALBERT: *(Offstage and in his most refined English.)* Well, I must thank you all for coming. It was really a very pleasant evening.

VOICE: *(Offstage.)* We enjoyed it, Albert. Really we did.

ALBERT: *(Offstage.)* A little dead and a bit reserved, but that's England for you.

(They all laugh.)

VOICE: *(Offstage.)* What time are you actually going?

ALBERT: *(Offstage.)* Well, my plane to freedom leaves at precisely nine hundred hours, Greenwich Mean Time. I soon gone for good. *(They all laugh again.)*

VOICE: *(Offstage.)* We'll miss you.

ALBERT: *(Offstage: aggressively and in patois.)* Don't gimme none yer nostalgia shit, man. I don't even pack up me bags yet. *(Laughter and nervous pause.)*

VOICE: *(Offstage.)* Well, we'd better leave you to it, then. Goodnight and good luck, Albert. Really, good luck. *(Pause. They leave and the door shuts.)*

ALBERT: *(Offstage.)* Goodnight and thank you again.

(RUTH is still in the garden. She tenses up and waits. After a moment ALBERT comes through into the conservatory. He stands behind her and looks at her. She in turn looks out blankly down the garden. RUTH knows he is there but she turns around too quickly. He comes down to meet her.)

RUTH: I didn't hear you come back in. Have they gone?

(She looks at him but he breaks the contact. Pause. She keeps looking at him. He moves further forward down the garden. He looks tired.)

ALBERT: *(Quietly.)* Bastards.

(RUTH moves forward to say something.)

(Quietly.)

They make me sick.

(Pause.)

Where they be, nuh? Where they be?

RUTH: Who?

ALBERT: Who? How long I been in this country?

RUTH: About...

ALBERT: No fucking 'about' about it. Nearly twenty-one years now.

RUTH: *(Moving off toward the dining room.)* I'll turn off the record player.

ALBERT: *(Quietly.)* Leave it.

(He pours himself a drink. It's a small glass of whisky. He overfills the glass and whisky spills all over the floor.) Lemme tell you...

RUTH: Albert, it's nearly one o'clock.

ALBERT: I say, lemme tell you or you is deaf or what? Nearly twenty-one years in this country and only eight people show up. Over ten years in social work and only three of the bastards manage to drag their arse around here. And my own son.

RUTH: He sent a telegram, Albert.

ALBERT: I know he send a telegram. I have it here in my pocket, OK? I know what a fucking telegram is.

(He takes it out, then scornfully:.)

'Will be late but will make it.'

(Repeating.)

'Will be late but will make it.' What he think it is, a quiz show or something? *(The record comes to an end and is stuck at the end of the track.)*

RUTH: I'd better see to the record.

(She does not move.) Albert?

ALBERT: I hear you. What you want me to do – carry you in?

(RUTH goes into the dining room. ALBERT sucks his teeth and steps on a piece of glass.) Shit!

(The glass goes through his sandal and cuts him. RUTH comes back through, having switched off the record player.)

RUTH: Are you all right?

ALBERT: A little bit of blood never hurt nobody. Is my neck they all want.

RUTH: Who, Albert?

ALBERT: *(Mimics.)* Who, Albert? Man came here with nothing. Look at me now. House, car…

(He breaks off suddenly.)

…this is the hottest night since I come here.

(He begins to peel off his shirt.)

All this time here and they have to save up the only tropical night for me last one. I probably get back there and find it snowing. *(Resigned.)*

World turn upside down.

RUTH: Shall I carry on packing?

ALBERT: What he say the woman call?

RUTH: Sonja.

ALBERT: Name like that the girl bound to be black. My son have a woman and he telling me, 'Will be late but will make it.' Him come a black man all right. So fucking inefficient. You know, is only two places a black man interested in turning up on time: a white woman's bedroom and the dinner table.

(They catch each other's eye. Pause.) You want a drink?

RUTH: Brandy please.

ALBERT: We have brandy? I never see none before.

RUTH: At the back there.

ALBERT: How long you have this?

RUTH: Ages. Didn't you see it?

ALBERT: Didn't you just hear me? I'm not stupid, woman. I know what brandy look like.

RUTH: Sorry.

(Pause.)

You think we ought to turn off the lights?

ALBERT: What? And sit out here in the dark?

RUTH: No, I thought we could go in the dining room.

ALBERT: What the hell for? For one, is a hot night out here, and for two, I don't have no more fucking electricity bills to pay in this country, so tonight I going to get me own back on them all arse.

(Pause. He drinks.)

I'd have never bothered coming here if I'd have realized that three-quarters of the money you work your backside off for you got to pay out just to keep a bit of heat in your damn body.

RUTH: It's not always cold.

ALBERT: You think I don't know that? I was making a generalization, all right? Sometimes I think you don't even got the brains to be a housewife.

(Pause.)

Look, if you going look like somebody put out a fire in your face with a size ten boot then maybe you better go and do some more packing or whatever it is you doing.

(Pause. He touches her lightly on the arm as if to say 'sorry'. He is tired. He gets up slowly and goes forward onto the grass. He bends and picks up a handful. It is almost a performance. He speaks reflectively and to himself.)

Grass and soil
Trouble and toil
Ina Inglan

Sky ain't blue
But neither are you
Ina Inglan

I make them up when I first come here.

(Pause.)

A traveller is a man of knowledge.

(RUTH sits and listens. She hears him talking to himself.)

Quiet! Even on a still night in England you can hear the sea. Listen!

(RUTH comes down to join him; they both listen.)

Why is it that the sea always sounds so fucking guilty? Whispering like it knows something but is not going say nothing. It just going keep on whispering. Listen.

(They listen.)

You finish packing?

(He is still listening.)

RUTH: Nearly.

ALBERT: You better go to sleep now before you meet yourself getting up in the morning.

RUTH: Are you sure?

ALBERT: Time in the morning to finish off.

RUTH: Goodnight, Albert.

(She kisses him on the cheek and moves to go off.)

ALBERT: *(To himself.)* Back home we have a saying: quickest way out the gutter to the hills is through London. *(RUTH stops and looks at him.)*

RUTH: Albert? Would you rather be on your own tonight?

(ALBERT does not hear her and he begins to wander off further down the garden.)

ALBERT: Soon be morning. A new day.

(Pause.)

Vince didn't show up either,

(Disillusioned.)

Didn't really expect him to.

(RUTH leaves him and goes inside. Clearly he isn't aware of her. ALBERT drops the grass and watches it spiral to the ground. As he does so the lighting on the house begins to fade, leaving him alone at the bottom of the garden.)

(A tape begins. ALBERT is in a street. We hear the sound of cars rushing past. It's a busy street. Now ALBERT is no longer alone. He is joined by MURIEL and she holds a baby in her arms. She is in her early twenties and is inadequately dressed for the cold: a short jacket and skirt, a light blouse, flat shoes and an ungainly flowered hat. She has brought on a large cardboard suitcase, which ALBERT picks up to carry, and she also has a package, which she gives to him; he tucks it under one arm. On the case is printed: 'MR & MRS A. WILLIAMS. ENGLAND'. They are cold. It is winter. They move out of the station and into the street. This is indicated by the soundtrack. They stand helplessly at the edge of the pavement, totally undecided as to whether to cross the road or what. MURIEL looks up at ALBERT.)

MURIEL: Albert?

(He can't answer. He doesn't look. He puts down the case. MURIEL looks at him still. She wants to cry. They stand there. ALBERT turns and takes the baby from her. He puts his arm around her.)

ALBERT: Muriel, England cold, nuh?

(From the other side of the road an older black man – VINCE – in a heavy overcoat and with a medal pinned to his lapel appears. He stands and looks at the pair of them and slowly approaches. A car sounds its horn at him as he crosses. He shouts after it.)

VINCE: And the same to you 'n' all, mate.

(ALBERT gives the baby back to MURIEL.)

You all lost?

ALBERT: No.

VINCE: But you just get off the boat?

ALBERT: Yes.

VINCE: You looks lost to me. Why you not take you wife and child out the cold nuh, man? England can be wicked for disease and all sorts of things, you know. I hear pneumonia and bronchitis and all them English disease is much worse than tropical ones but I can't know for sure for me wrap up well as you can see. You going have to buy a scarf, you realize that?

ALBERT: Yes.

VINCE: Come, let's have a cup of tea in here.

(They pause.)

What happen, you don't trust me?

ALBERT: No... Yes...

VINCE: You ever drink English tea before?

ALBERT: Yes...well, not real English tea.

MURIEL: Yes we have.

ALBERT: But not in England.

VINCE: Come.

(They go into a café, which is represented by a table and three chairs. Fade out the soundtrack of the street as they enter. They sit.)

Look man, you ever hear of self-service?

ALBERT: I don't think so.

VINCE: Well, is easy. No waiter or nothing, you know. No barman.

(He waits for them to get up but they don't.)

Look, you just wait here and I go get us the tea.

(ALBERT digs into his pocket. VINCE holds back his arm.)
No man, you is the guest.

(He goes to get the tea.)

MURIEL: Do you think we should let him?

ALBERT: I don't know.

(He takes the baby from her and wipes the baby's mouth carefully with his handkerchief. Then MURIEL takes the handkerchief and blows her nose with it. She wipes her eyes which are still a little damp.)

Still cold?

MURIEL: No.

(VINCE arrives back with the tea on a tray.)

VINCE: Here we are.

(He puts the tray down.)

By the way, I'm Vincent. Vince.

ALBERT: Albert. Albert Williams.

(They shake hands.)

My wife, Muriel Williams.

(They shake hands.)

Our son, Remi.

VINCE: How old is he?

MURIEL: Three months now.

ALBERT: Is a new life for the boy.

VINCE: He won't regret it.

MURIEL: We hope not.

VINCE: You have anywhere to stay?

ALBERT: Well not yet but...

VINCE: Thought not. I see you all standing at the side of the road like you is lamppost or something. Too many coloured people coming here now with no planning and thing.

ALBERT: Are there really that many here?

(VINCE laughs.)

VINCE: Thousands. Hundreds of thousands and they all running down the wrong road. My grandfather always tell me, 'Son, when you leave the island' – for he know I going do so eventually – everyone does – he tell me, 'Make sure you blasted well bring back a piece of the country with you when you return.' All over the Caribbean you hear old men talking about when they was in America or Costa Rica or Cuba or Panama or wherever the hell, and all of them come back with nothing – all poor immigrants who can never make it. All they got is their honesty. In an ideal world them all deserve honesty and money for most of them did labour for it. Seems they can't get both.

(Pause.)

Well, I know what you is wanting to ask. I come here in the war at the time when a Frenchman in England was exotic. RAF pilot.

MURIEL: I noticed the medal.

VINCE: Is nothing. Nearly everyone who finish get one.

ALBERT: Back home a medal like that make you famous.

VINCE: But it can't buy me food. England going teach you practicalities. I been here nearly eighteen years now and I don't own much more than what you see I have on my back. Life begins with the shilling and ends with it. Me, I don't have enough shillings.

(Pause.)

I'm a natural-born businessman – administrator – but is like being the last unicorn in the world. Is nothing you can do about it. You going die and there going be nothing left to show for it. Don't matter how much you try, you just don't got the technology. *(Pause.)*

You don't have nowhere to stay? *(ALBERT shakes his head.)*

Is just what I mean. You think it easy for a coloured man to get a room in England? And with a wife and baby too?

(He leans closer.)

'Nigger whore, fuck off home and take your picknie with you.' 'Sambo, get back on your jam jar.'

(Pause.)

In England is legal law to put up a sign saying, 'No coloureds in this house' or just 'No monkeys'. People back home is crazy, you know. They writing and telling you all the wrong things about England. All the things that don't really concern you. I not saying is not possible to make it here. All I saying is it hard. You all better stop by me. Mulatto man upstairs pack up his bags yesterday and gone off to Sweden or Norway or some nonsense place, to play jazz he say. Noise of the man's trumpet driving everyone mad. I fix it up with the landlord – old Jewish man – it not cheap though.

MURIEL: We've got some money if you…

(She reaches for the money.)

VINCE: You just hang on to your money. You going need it.

(They get up to leave and move out into the street. Tape of the noise of cars starts up again.)

(To ALBERT.) You going freeze up to death less you buy some new clothes.

(He looks around.)

It soon going rain and in England it don't rain hard and hot, you know. Is like a dog pissing down your leg.

(Pause.)

We get a bus, settle Muriel and the baby in, then we better think about getting a job. You have a trade?

ALBERT: No.

VINCE: Then you probably going be seeing a lot more buses.

(To MURIEL.)

Come dear, less you want your child preserve in a block of ice. On a day like this I see women in this country who have to take up a hammer and chisel to chip the nappy off their baby backside.

(They drift off and leave ALBERT alone on stage.)

(The lights begin to change back to the present.)

ALBERT: *(Incredulously: he doesn't understand.)* I probably going be seeing a lot more buses?

(He turns to go back up the garden, RUTH, in her dressing gown, comes through the conservatory and down the garden. It's as if he doesn't recognize her at first. Then his mind clears and he moves toward her.)

RUTH: It's late, Albert. You must sleep.

ALBERT: Too late.

RUTH: For what?

ALBERT: Everything.

(Pause.)

RUTH: Are you coming to bed?

ALBERT: Go to bed.

RUTH: Albert, why don't you talk to me? Why don't you talk to me like you used to? You talk to me these days as if you've got an audience to please and I'm just a 'feed', a straight man or something.

ALBERT: A straight woman.

RUTH: Please Albert, I'm trying to talk to you, to communicate… I don't want to go to bed alone… Not tonight. It's late.

ALBERT: I see. You feeling hot. You want me come and see to you tonight? Is that what you think of me?

RUTH: I want you to care for me. I know you're busy but you did care for me once, didn't you?

ALBERT: Yes, I cared for you. You listened to me.

RUTH: Yes, I listened to you because you talked to me. I listened when you told me about your father being a cane-cutter and your mother selling peanuts at the side of the road, and you listened to me when I told you about my parents being relics from an Edwardian age when raising girls was tantamount to raising children for strangers, a waste of time, and I saw the real emotion in your eyes, Albert, when you asked me to marry you. And that was in that grubby little bedsitter full of social work pamphlets and old copies of *New Society*. If only you could be bothered to talk to me I'd listen to you, today, tomorrow, anytime, or have I outgrown my usefulness?

ALBERT: No.

RUTH: Well, I feel as if I have. Please be honest. Just tell me.

ALBERT: I going come to bed. I join you there.

(Pause.)

RUTH: Please don't be too long. And talk to me. I am your wife.

ALBERT: *(Without looking at her.)* Is there I going join you.

(RUTH goes, ALBERT looks at all the lights hanging from the trees, etc. Then he moves down the garden again as if he wants his memory to be dislodged. He is very confused. Enter REMI from the dining room with a holdall shoulder bag. He is twenty-one, dressed in tidy jeans and a jacket. He even has on a collar and tie. He puts down the bag and comes forward into the conservatory. For a few moments he just stands and watches his father who peers into the darkness. Then he moves down to the garden.)

REMI: Dad?

(ALBERT does not turn round.)

Is it all over?

(No answer from ALBERT.) I'm sorry I was late.

ALBERT: You weren't late. You just weren't here that's all. It's finished. You can be late for something that's still going on. If it's finished then you can't be late, boy. You just didn't show up.

REMI: *(Coming down toward him.)* I got the first train I could.

(ALBERT turns toward him.)

ALBERT: What happen? British Rail only running one train a day? Midnight Express?

REMI: No but…

ALBERT: No but fucking nothing. Since you old enough to switch on your ears I done been telling you black people in this country must act and feel like a tribe or they not going survive. But what fucking use is a tribe if nobody taking any notice of the elders them?

REMI: I don't know.

ALBERT: When you think you going see me again?

(Pause.)

Boy, is a farewell party, not anniversary or baptism or any other damn nonsense.

REMI: I'm sorry.

ALBERT: Sorry? And where the bitch you say you going bring? She gone off or maybe she not want to meet your family.

REMI: I don't know.

ALBERT: What you mean, you don't know?

REMI: I don't know where she is. I was supposed to meet her at the station at about seven o'clock but she never came. I waited a bit then started to ring round. I couldn't find her. I sent you a telegram 'cause the line was constantly engaged. I suppose it was people ringing you up and telling you what time they were arriving and all the rest.

(Pause.)

By the time I gave up waiting for her it was nearly twelve so I thought I'd get the train without her and just catch the end of the party.

ALBERT: The bitch stood you up. Me arse.

(He takes a drink.)

REMI: She's not a bitch.

ALBERT: So what make she so special? She Marilyn Monroe or what?

REMI: No.

ALBERT: She white?

REMI: No.

ALBERT: Suppose you think you got something real special now you find yourself a black woman.

(REMI starts to walk away.)

Stand still when I talk to you! What the fuck is this? You telling me you can't make it to Ruth and myself going-away party because of some stupid little black bitch?

REMI: She's not a bitch, she's a woman.

ALBERT: Women piss in the bath, ladies get out and use the toilet. What is she?

REMI: *(Less aggressively.)* She's a woman.

ALBERT: *(Easy.)* Boy, you too young, you know.

REMI: I'm not.

ALBERT: You think twenty-one is old or something?

REMI: Old enough.

ALBERT: Old enough for what? You want to fight with me, a man? You want to do my job? You want to fuck my women? You done nothing till you have your pieces of paper for me to see – you done nothing and you are nothing till I see a degree in front of me.

REMI: Well, then, I'll always be nothing.

ALBERT: You trying to come clever with me?

REMI: I'll always be nothing in your eyes. I'm not going back to University next year.

ALBERT: Don't be fucking stupid. If I have to stay here and physically take you there you going back. Whether you like it or not.

REMI: I've got to get a job. I'm getting married. Sonja's pregnant and I'm going to marry her.

ALBERT: Don't talk fucking stupidness to me, boy.

REMI: I'm going to marry her.

ALBERT: Over my dead body.

REMI: All right.

(Pause, ALBERT pours REMI a drink and gives it to him. He changes his tone.)

ALBERT: Boy, you still don't know the difference between a black woman and a white woman.

(He sits down.)

Tell me about this woman, then. She have any form? Fast finisher, firm ground, like a heavy jockey, or maybe the bitch tell you is she first time out.

REMI: She's not a bitch.

ALBERT: How you know is your child?

REMI: It is.

ALBERT: And even if it is – which is never definite – how it is you can't let she go to work and you finish off your education?

REMI: We need money more than we need a piece of paper.

ALBERT: And I bet you she need a man more than she need a baby.

(Pause. They look at each other.)

You can't control yourself? You can't use protection, self-discipline? You can't listen to what I tell you?

REMI: When I was twelve you gave me a book on the sex life of a banana fly. It mentioned a dog on the last page and anyhow, protection don't always work.

ALBERT: *(Shouting.)* But fucking self-discipline does; now use some self-discipline, stop acting like a frigging arsehole and tell she to fuck off out your life. Twenty-one and you want to let a fucking pregnant woman hold you back. Only reason I get your mother pregnant is because I know her father going give out the money for us all to come to England. I can't see no other way I going to get here. There has to be a reason for everything; is just common sense. You don't realize yet that the white man is like a storm of rain trying to wash us away. Piss on us at will. But I fight back. Now, after everything, after I can rest up me umbrella for a while, you think I going let a black woman shit upon my head or the head of my son? They like black social workers, you know, is why I decide is not law or medicine or any of those things I going try for when your mother leave the both of us alone in this fucking country. I decide is social work for me for I know they like nothing better than having black people explaining black people to them. It makes them feel like they is important or something. But you think they like black drop-outs, black nothings?

(He laughs.)

Once you is that, boy, they going piss on you for true.

REMI: We're getting married next week.

ALBERT: Boy, you don't be marrying anybody. I already done explain why.

REMI: That's just it, you say you explain but you don't take any time over it because you're too busy with other things. And when you do talk to me you reduce me to being some sort of small helpless pawn in some game in which, like you, you can only win if you don't let 'the white man' push you about, but I don't really think it's like that. All your friends and stuff are white, your wife's white.

ALBERT: Boy, what you trying to say to me?

REMI: It can't all be a game, a hustle. It can't all be that straightforward.

ALBERT: Boy, life in England don't be no game: is war, you hear?

(They stare at each other, ALBERT breaks the spell.) Where this black woman be?

REMI: She's an orphan, so this afternoon she went to the orphanage she used to stay at to get her birth certificate and things. *(Pause.)*

She needs them before she can get married.

ALBERT: Boy, are you my son? The same hot seed I spilled that dark night?

REMI: I don't know.

(ALBERT smashes REMI across the face and knocks him over.)

ALBERT: You filthy little bastard. The mistake I make with you is thinking too much about you – caring too much. Back home you'd have been living with your grandmother, my mother. She'd have knocked some fucking sense into your head.

REMI: *(Slowly getting up.)* I don't care what you say any more.

ALBERT: You're a pathetic sight. A man? You a man, boy? A man stands and fights, he doesn't just fall over. A man will give as good as he gets. A man won't let no woman, no little girl, trap him like he is a fucking fly. You feel like a man?

REMI: I feel right.

ALBERT: You feel like a man?

REMI: I feel right.

ALBERT: You feel like a man?

REMI: No!

ALBERT: Well, fuck off out my house till you feel like a man for I don't want to leave no twenty-one-year-old boy in this fucking country. You think I get where I am today, Executive Social Worker and Magistrate, by being a fucking boy? You think I have this house, two cars and a flat by being a boy? You think a boy can afford to throw parties like the ones I throw? Invitations all around the place? Well? Well?

REMI: I don't know.

ALBERT: No, you don't know. You don't know what any damn fool can tell you for straight and that is that your responsibility is to yourself and your education, so just tell she to fuck off, boy, or take your boy arse out of me sight. Go! Go on, fuck off! I don't work me arse off for you for twenty-odd years to listen to this shit. Fuck off!

(REMI goes off to the dining room. He goes to take his bag but he leaves it and goes off without it. ALBERT pours a drink. He is still fuming mad.)

(We enter ALBERT's mind. We hear the sound of a night club. Laughter. Then a woman's voice cuts across the noise.)

VOICE: Albert?

(ALBERT puts down his drink.)

ALBERT: Well, say what you got to say, then.

VOICE: I was going to write but I'm not too good at it. I'm sorry to have to come down here in front of your friends.

ALBERT: Well, speak up then, nuh.

VOICE: I don't want you to marry me but I need money.

ALBERT: Money for what?

VOICE: You know what. The baby.

ALBERT: Just fuck off.

(RUTH comes through from the dining room, unseen by ALBERT. She still has on her dressing gown. The noise of the club fades away.)

RUTH: Albert?

ALBERT: I said fuck off, bitch.

RUTH: Albert, it's me.

ALBERT: Mother?

RUTH: Ruth.

ALBERT: Ruth?

(He turns to face her.)

RUTH: Are you all right?

ALBERT: My son's still growing up.

(Pause.)

The grave of many cherished dreams, London Transport.

(Pause.)

Maybe he wants to go and work on the fucking buses.

RUTH: Will he be back?

ALBERT: I going look for him. He's not working no fucking buses.

(He picks up his drink and finishes it in one.)

RUTH: He's young still.

ALBERT: Finish your packing if you want. I got a journey to make. Mango ripe yet?

RUTH: What mangoes?

ALBERT: Mango at the bottom of the garden. *(Pause.)*

They ripe yet? They either fall off or get picked off. Wonder what they do to them over in England. I going look.

(He moves off down the garden and again stands and stares into the darkness. He is beyond RUTH.)

RUTH: Come to bed, Albert please. I'm getting cold. Albert?

ALBERT: I going look for him.

RUTH: Look, wait there. I'll just go and get you your tablets.

(He is not responding so she turns slowly and goes back inside. As soon as she has gone ALBERT speaks.)

ALBERT: I don't have no trade but I going do my best to look after she and the child when we gets to England.

(We begin to hear the strains of some crackly calypso music of the fifties. A bar is wheeled on. ALBERT is in a cellar night club. It is quite dark and already a place of faded dreams. VINCE throws a towel at him and ALBERT catches it and begins to wipe the table.)

VINCE: First night. Business bound to pick up.

ALBERT: I hope so otherwise it looks like we going bankrupt.

VINCE: Word just not get around yet. I tell you is enough West Indians in this country to support a business venture of this kind.

ALBERT: We have to work out a rota because for the next few weeks I going be working evening shift.

VINCE: Things will pick up and you soon give up the buses.

ALBERT: I hope so otherwise they going start finding out we not just smart collar and tie and friendly service with a big banana smile. They too fucking prejudiced and some white man going die in my arms before long. Death on the number thirty-eight.

VINCE: Take it easy, Albert.

(Pause.)

How's Muriel and the baby? I don't see them for a while now.

ALBERT: All right, I suppose. Country cold, man. Staying in bed a lot.

VINCE: I think we should advertise a bit more.

(Footsteps.)

Sounds like a customer.

ALBERT: I hope so. Is nearly midnight.

(In walks LYNN. She is white, in her late twenties. She wears old but clean clothes. She is not on the game or about to be. VINCE gets up.)

VINCE: Pleased to meet you. Welcome to the Tropical Club.

LYNN: I heard the music. Is it private?

VINCE: No dear. Is our first night. A night club for the masses.

LYNN: *(Looking around.)* I see.

(Pause.)

You sell drinks, then?

ALBERT: Tonight, drinks on the house.

VINCE: What would you like?

LYNN: I'll have a rum, if that's all right, please.

VINCE: A rum it is, and why not, is Tropical Club. You like the music?

LYNN: Yeah. Great.

VINCE: Take a seat.

(She sits down.)

You don't like it, we change it, no problem.

LYNN: No, it's great. I really like it. *(VINCE goes to get the drink.)* Is he the manager, then?

ALBERT: We both are. We own the club. A new country. A new investment.

LYNN: Oh, so you're not from round here, then?

ALBERT: Caribbean.

LYNN: Oh, yeah. Yeah, thought so.

VINCE: Three glasses and a bottle. We might as well all have one.

(He pours the drinks.)

LYNN: It'll keep out the cold.

VINCE: Is true. Is true. Cheers.

LYNN: Cheers.

ALBERT: Cheers.

LYNN: So this is your job, then? You must be quite well-off.

ALBERT: I work in transportation economics.

LYNN: My ex-husband worked on the buses. Driver. Number seventy-three route. We've just split up. Horrible living in a bedsit, though I don't suppose either of you'll know anything about that.

VINCE: Oh, don't be so sure about…

ALBERT: I've heard about it.

LYNN: Not nice, I can tell you that for nothing.

ALBERT: I'm Albert. This is my partner, Vince.

LYNN: *(Shaking hands.)* Pleased to meet you. I'm Lynn.
I suppose we'll be seeing more of each other as this
place'll really take off, won't it?

VINCE: We hope so.

LYNN: Do you know the people in the house upstairs?

VINCE: Is a young West Indian couple. Small baby girl.

LYNN: Don't they mind the noise? Lights were still on when
I came down.

ALBERT: They only own the house. The basement is our
property.

LYNN: I see.

ALBERT: Maybe we better close up for tonight.

VINCE: Tomorrow I going do some advertising.

ALBERT: Can we walk you home? Is late.

LYNN: Thank you.

ALBERT: *(To VINCE.)* Just leave the bottles and glasses
and them there, boy. We can wash and clean them up
tomorrow before we open. *(VINCE takes the things to
the bar.)*

LYNN: It's nice music.

(Pause.)

Why is it coloured people always dance as if they've got
one foot nailed to the floor?

ALBERT: As if what?

LYNN: You know, like this.

(She demonstrates. VINCE has already put the bottle and glasses back. He looks on as does ALBERT.)

ALBERT: Well, I suppose some do.

(To VINCE.)

Shut off the music and lights then we ready, boy.

(VINCE picks up his hat. He obediently shuts off the lights and the music. The three of them leave and move out into the street.)

VINCE: *(To LYNN.)* So how far is it, then?

ALBERT: *(To VINCE.)* I going see you tomorrow, then.

VINCE: What you mean you going see me tomorrow?

ALBERT: You not opening up, or what?

VINCE: Yes but…

ALBERT: Yes but then I going see you tomorrow.

(VINCE waits for a moment then realizes he's not wanted.)

VINCE: Goodnight.

LYNN: Goodnight.

(VINCE shuffles off.)

ALBERT: Is cold, nuh?

LYNN: Well, I don't really feel it much though I used to get chilblains when I was a girl.

ALBERT: But you still look like a girl to me.

LYNN: Get off, flattery'll get you nowhere.

(ALBERT goes back into the club and turns on lights and music, LYNN follows him in. He stands, watches her then moves toward her and past her as lights fade in the club.)

(He moves toward MURIEL who is sitting on a chair alone with the baby at the other side of the stage. She is dressed for bed.)

ALBERT: So what happen? You all right?

MURIEL: No.

ALBERT: No? Baby all right?

MURIEL: I said 'no'.

ALBERT: So what you want me to do? Is only 'no' you have in your dictionary?

MURIEL: You working till now? Till this time?

ALBERT: I got something to tell you.

MURIEL: You going to take your jacket off?

ALBERT: I say I got something to tell you, I don't need to undress to make my mouth work.

(She does not respond.)

You remember the money we bring over for buying a house? *(No response.)*

You remember the money?

MURIEL: The money my dead mother leave for me.

ALBERT: The same.

(No answer. He has to carry on.) I done invest it.

(Pause.)

You got nothing to say?

(She stares hard at him.)

(Lights fade and he goes across to the club.)

LYNN: You look tired.

ALBERT: I work hard.

LYNN: You've never had it easy, have you? I can see that.

ALBERT: Who does?

(Lights fade and he goes back across to MURIEL who is standing with the baby. They are in the middle of a row.)

ALBERT: You can't talk to me?

MURIEL: About what?

ALBERT: Anything.

MURIEL: Like my dead mother money?

ALBERT: So why you keep bringing that up? Is an old story.

(No answer.)

Look, why you keep looking at me like I thief it?

MURIEL: I want to go home.

ALBERT: Home what?

MURIEL: Home home!

ALBERT: So how many times must I tell you this is England, entertainment business, and things picking up, so why you can't frigging see that, eh? Why you can't assist me, support me, instead of just digging me up with your mouth, day in, day out?

MURIEL: You, a big man, asking me for support when you thief off the money and leave your wife and child in...

ALBERT: I don't leave you or nobody! I done invest the money for the future, our future, and the future of my son…

MURIEL: Albert, what the…?

ALBERT: Albert, what the fucking nothing! You make me so damn angry for you don't listen, you don't learn from the country, you don't study or nothing! You just sit here with the boy and not a scrap of ambition about your body. Just nothing! Nothing!

(Lights fade and ALBERT moves back across to the club.)

LYNN: All right?

ALBERT: Sure, sure.

LYNN: It's just that you look like you should be somewhere else, like your mind's wandering.

ALBERT: Me? No, I sometimes promise to keep an eye on some kids whose parents got to work nights, but is all right tonight. You see, it's tough on a lot of us West Indians coming here. Not enough money for babysitters and all we family is back in the Caribbean.

LYNN: You sure you don't have to stop by them tonight? I won't mind.

ALBERT: No, no. No problem at all.

LYNN: I see. So you never got married then?

(ALBERT laughs.)

ALBERT: Me? No, I love my freedom too much.

(Pause.)

But I like you.

LYNN: I bet you say that to all the ladies.

(Enter RUTH into the conservatory as lights go up on the house. She is holding a glass of water and a couple of tablets. She pauses a moment then walks down the garden toward ALBERT. She hears him talking to himself.)

ALBERT: No man, not me. That I love them, yes, but I never said I liked one before.

(LYNN leads the way off, glancing over her shoulder and encouraging ALBERT to follow. He stands, smiling broadly, and watches her go. RUTH puts her hand on ALBERT's shoulder.)

RUTH: Albert, you're shaking. Come inside.

ALBERT: *(Still smiling and looking to where LYNN has gone off.)* Is cold out here.

(Pause. The smile falls from his face.) I did wrong by she. I did wrong.

(Pause.)

I did wrong by a lot of people.

RUTH: You're just tired, Albert.

ALBERT: But I can't sleep tonight, not tonight. I done finish with sleep.

RUTH: But you must sleep otherwise…

ALBERT: Jesus Christ Almighty, I'm scared, Ruth. I scared like I never did be scared before.

RUTH: Of what?

ALBERT: Everything! I never depended on nobody in my life since I come here. Nobody at all but now I don't feel so good. I must be getting old.

RUTH: But I'll help you, Albert.

ALBERT: You help me? I have my pride still, you know. You think I can lower myself to asking you for help?

RUTH: You don't have to ask, just accept, but ever since I've known you you've had this childish view of life as some kind of market place where if you take something you have to give something back, but you don't have to at all. You must learn how to accept, Albert. For my sake too.

ALBERT: Sometimes I don't know why you put up with me.

RUTH: *(Half under her breath.)* I won't put up with you forever, Albert. I'm not strong enough.

ALBERT: So when you going stop 'putting up with me'?

RUTH: When I don't think I can help you any more.

ALBERT: I see.

(Pause.)

So you going leave me too. Like my son. I sometimes wish I could just walk out on everything. Be a complete bastard like everyone thinks I am. Just give up on everything. But not even I can do it. Not even me.

(Pause.)

I do some wrong things in my time but I'm not an evil man, Ruth. I'm not totally without understanding.

RUTH: I know you're not…

ALBERT: I could have left the baby in a children's home, you know that! Or I could have let his mother take him back home with her. I could have made her take him back, but no, I want that child with me. I want that child to have a better education. A chance. *(He laughs.)*

A marriage mash-up and the father want the son. Is an old story. You know I love that boy so bad I can't even talk to him. He just tell me as much. I find myself talking to him like he is competing with me or something, like he's a threat to me and it hurts me, man. It gets to me.

Sometimes I forget is my own flesh and blood I talking to.

(Pause.)

Go to bed, Ruth, just leave me alone now.

RUTH: Albert…

ALBERT: Don't talk to me, please! I going rest a minute then I going out to find my son. I going walk the streets. Like a tracker dog I come…

(He laughs lightly.)

I going get out my old boy scout tenderfoot badge, pin it on, and start roaming the streets for the boy. At my age! *(RUTH wanders back up the garden and into the house, ALBERT shakes his head and paces nervously.)* At my age!

(The following dialogue between MURIEL and the NURSE is on tape and in ALBERT's mind.)

NURSE: Just a little harder, Muriel, a little harder.

ALBERT: *(Remembering.)* Just a little harder, Muriel, a little harder.

(HUSTON walks over to join ALBERT, who sees him now. He pushes a bunch of flowers into ALBERT's hand and begins to pace and puff on a cigarette nervously.)

NURSE: Once more, Muriel, just once more, dear.

MURIEL: I can't.

NURSE: Yes you can. Once more.

(MURIEL moans.)

That's it.

(The baby begins to cry and HUSTON stops pacing. MURIEL cries.)

Relax, dear, it's a boy. A healthy baby boy. There we are. Would you like to see your visitors? *(The baby begins to cry out loud again.)*

MURIEL: What's the matter? What's the matter with him?

NURSE: It's only natural, Muriel. Don't worry.

(The NURSE enters. She comes out to meet the two of them, MURIEL is wheeled in on a hospital trolley.)

NURSE: Mr Stewart. Mr Williams.

(She ushers the two men over to the trolley, first making HUSTON stub out his cigarette. ALBERT lingers behind a little. HUSTON rushes straight to his daughter.)

HUSTON: Where my grandson?

NURSE: How do you know it's a boy?

(HUSTON spins round.)

Well it is, but there was an alternative.

ALBERT: *(To the NURSE.)* Is she all right?

NURSE: Perfectly.

(She takes the flowers and puts them in a jar. HUSTON picks up the baby and holds him aloft.)

HUSTON: My boy.

NURSE: Mr Stewart. Please. Go easy.

MURIEL: Albert?

(ALBERT steps forward and takes her hand.)

ALBERT: How are you?

MURIEL: Oh, Albert, you do ask some stupid questions.

(She squeezes his hand weakly with both of hers. HUSTON drifts out into the centre of the stage and holds the baby close. He is totally taken with the child.)

HUSTON: A son.

NURSE: *(To MURIEL.)* Your husband brought you some flowers. I'll put them by the bed.

(She sets them down.)

MURIEL: You shouldn't have, Albert.

ALBERT: It was no trouble really, I just passing the shop and went in.

MURIEL: Nurse, can I have some water?

NURSE: Yes dear.

MURIEL: *(With increased urgency.)* Some water, please!

NURSE: Relax.

(She pours some water from the jug and gives it to MURIEL.)

Look, perhaps you men had best leave now. All this excitement isn't good for her. *(HUSTON turns, still holding the child.)*

HUSTON: Leave? Already? We only just come in.

NURSE: You can come again tomorrow. I'm afraid your daughter needs to sleep more than she needs visitors. *(The NURSE comes across and takes the baby and carries him back to MURIEL.)*

ALBERT: Short and sweet. I'll see you tomorrow then.

(He kisses MURIEL and the baby.)

MURIEL: I'll be here.

(She smiles weakly.)

HUSTON: *(Pensive.)* You make sure you look after yourself, girl.

(He gives her a peck on the cheek.)

MURIEL: I will.

(The trolley is wheeled off.)

HUSTON: *(To the NURSE.)* Look after she good. I paying real money out to you and it don't grow on trees, you know.

NURSE: Nothing to worry about, Mr Stewart. You can both come back tomorrow.

(They are both ushered into the centre of the stage by the NURSE. She goes off to MURIEL and the baby. ALBERT and HUSTON stand and face each other. ALBERT is nervous. He wants to have a drink and unwind, HUSTON is worried.)

HUSTON: Is a fine son you have.

ALBERT: I know.

(Pause.)

HUSTON: I don't want that boy brought up on this island. As soon as Muriel is better I going give you the money to take she and the child off to England. You can't say I didn't warn you.

(Pause.)

My grandson…your son…belongs to England. You hear me?

ALBERT: Yes sir.

HUSTON: It make me sick to have to do it but you want him to be like us, me a third-class shopkeeper, you a groom and labourer? *(ALBERT shakes his head.)*

Is all I got to say on the matter.

(Moving to go off.)

What you going call him?

ALBERT: Remi.

HUSTON: *(Reflectively.)* Remi.

ALBERT: Remi Huston.

(HUSTON is obviously touched. He moves off.)

HUSTON: Remi Huston… Remi Huston Williams.

(Harder and to ALBERT.)

The child belongs to England.

(HUSTON goes off and leaves ALBERT alone on stage. The lights on the house begin to brighten again, ALBERT is back home in the present. He looks around.)

ALBERT: Remi Huston… Remi Huston Williams.

(He moves off toward the house.)

I going find him, I going find my son.

END OF ACT ONE

Act Two

It is about three-thirty in the morning. RUTH is still in her dressing gown and putting something in the dustbin. She busies herself in the garden, SONJA enters, RUTH does not see her. SONJA is about twenty-one, black, and good-looking; trendy but not flashy, RUTH picks up some potted plants. She puts them down to do something else first and turns round and sees SONJA, which makes her jump.

RUTH: You gave me a fright.

SONJA: I'm Sonja. Remi's girlfriend.

RUTH: *(Catching her breath.)* I'm Ruth. I didn't know you'd arrived.

SONJA: I've just got here. A newcomer to the party.

(Pause.)

Remi's told me about you.

RUTH: Well, I hope it wasn't too bad.

(SONJA does not answer.)

Was the door open?

SONJA: Yes, I closed it in.

RUTH: Thank you. *(Pause.)* Albert, Remi's father, he's gone for a walk. He must have left it open. Sit down if you like. I'll get you a drink in a second. *(She starts packing things up.)*

I think Remi's gone with him too. I don't think he'll be long.

(Pause.)

SONJA: It's all over, then?

RUTH: The party?

SONJA: No, this. His father. Back home.

RUTH: You could say that. It had to at some point.

SONJA: So you're becoming a West Indian?

RUTH: Yes. I suppose I am in a sense.

(Pause.)

Do you mind if I continue to pack?

SONJA: No.

(RUTH continues to pack, holding up objects and putting them on the respective piles.)

RUTH: Plastic flowers, somebody gave them to Albert.

SONJA: Most black people are brought up with plastic flowers all around them. I've seen them all. Crocheted coverlets, unused sets of commemorative china, too much furniture, cars with cushions in the back seats, heavy clumsy ice buckets with designs so tasteless they make you want to roll over and die, but eventually you learn to stop making excuses for what you are. *(Embarrassed pause. SONJA looks dizzy.)*

RUTH: Are you feeling all right?

SONJA: I feel sick.

RUTH: You might as well get some sleep if you feel sick. There's only me to talk to.

SONJA: You don't think I'm good enough to talk to?

RUTH: No, I thought I might be boring you, that's all.

(Pause.)

Would you like a drink now?

SONJA: No.

RUTH: Well, if you do want anything just ask. I don't think Remi will be long.

(Pause.)

SONJA: Why's he going back?

RUTH: Retirement. He's earned it. He's been under a lot of pressure lately.

SONJA: Successful black man in Community Relations Circus.

(Pause.)

Fear. Is he frightened of something?

RUTH: I don't understand you.

SONJA: Why are you going?

RUTH: He's my husband. I love him and…

SONJA: I know, 'one day I'll discover…' and on, and on.

RUTH: Well, wouldn't you go if it was Remi?

SONJA: I'm not programmed by any man to do anything. I love with my head. I suppose it's what you get for being brought up in an orphanage. An overkeen sense of survival.

RUTH: I see, I didn't know.

(Pause.)

SONJA: You've got no choice really, have you?

RUTH: Albert's under pressure and things haven't been as…

(She stammers and stops, and takes her eyes from SONJA.)

SONJA: Don't you have anybody else to talk to?

RUTH: Sorry?

(Enter REMI. He ignores them and goes for a drink.) Hello.

(REMI grunts a reply.)

Did you see your father? He went out to look for you.

REMI: No.

(To SONJA.)

How long have you been here?

SONJA: Not long.

(RUTH is uncomfortable with both of them watching her.)

RUTH: I'll finish this off later.

(She goes, SONJA is agitated. She waits for REMI to make a move toward her. He watches RUTH go off. He takes his drink and then comes to her.)

REMI: What happened to you?

SONJA: I'm sorry but I had to stay.

REMI: What do you mean you had to stay? You could have at least come and told me you didn't want to come to the party.

SONJA: I did want to come to the party but...

REMI: But what?

SONJA: But I couldn't. I went back to the orphanage. It was an effort to do that I can tell you. But, I needed the birth certificate so up the steps and into the hall. Still stunk of disinfectant. Cold walls and floor. High ceilings. Impenetrable doors. Down the corridor to the warden's

office. Knock. Enter. I know that face. Jones. Sandra
Jones. Sonja Jones. Jones. Birth certificate. What for?
Marriage. Twenty-one now. No questions. Just one thing,
Jones. Your mother had a cousin over here with her. She
left a few things for you along with some of your parents'
belongings. They're in a small suitcase. I'll fetch them.
I thought my parents died in a fire. Can't have been much
left. Had to be a small suitcase really. Here it is. I could
sense it. This was going to be important. I sent you the
telegram.

REMI: Why didn't you come and bring the case with you?

SONJA: It was my parents' life – all that I had left. I wanted to
look at it on my own.

REMI: And what was there?

SONJA: Normal stuff. Bits of tin jewellery. An old bible. A-Z
of London. A map of England. Old photos of people I
don't know. And a pile of newspaper cuttings.

REMI: So?

SONJA: So I wanted to be with them. It's as close to my
parents as I've ever been, don't you understand that?
Suddenly your father's party wasn't very important.

REMI: But what about me? I waited for you and I missed the
party. I worried myself sick.

SONJA: I'm sorry but I'm here now.

(Pause.)

Well, I can go again, Remi, if you want me to.

REMI: Course I don't want you to go. It's just him.

SONJA: Who?

REMI: My father.

SONJA: What about him?

REMI: He isn't going to let us get married.

SONJA: What you mean he isn't going to let us? He can't stop us.

(REMI looks away.)

For God's sake, we're over twenty-one now. Are you waiting for him to change your nappy, or what?

REMI: I don't want to upset him at this stage.

SONJA: What stage?

REMI: Just before he retires.

SONJA: Runs off more like.

REMI: From what? He's got nothing to run from.

SONJA: People like him have always got something to run from. Usually themselves.

REMI: You can't say that about my father. You've never met him.

SONJA: Have you seen the look in that woman's face? She looks shell-shocked, like a survivor from World War Two. I only need to look at her to see him.

REMI: He means well, you know. Or else why would he stay with her all this time? He's in a bad way. He's deliberately going right back to where he started from. Not many people can do that and it must all seem like a bad dream, to him.

SONJA: Where did she get her bruises from? Fell over and hit her head against the side of the chair?

REMI: What bruises?

SONJA: Try looking past the image of your father's halo next time and you'll see them.

REMI: He doesn't hit her.

SONJA: How would you know? If you want to follow him lemming-like, then leave me out of it. 'He isn't going to let us get married'.

REMI: Look, I've just been for a walk and I've been thinking. I still want us to get married, you know that, but maybe he's right. In the long run we might need my degree. I'm sure he'd lend us the money to get by next year if we wanted.

SONJA: You ever think of changing your name to Faustus, daddy's boy? Anything for a bit of peace and quiet.

REMI: Don't call me boy.

SONJA: Well, stop acting like one! Are you just trying to please him?

REMI: I'll act how I fucking like!

SONJA: Well, you better take this.

(She takes off her engagement ring and holds it out.)

I got a return ticket and I know my way to the station.

REMI: Don't be stupid. Put it back on.

(SONJA throws the ring at REMI and it lands on the floor.)

SONJA: So give it to your father.

REMI: Pick it up.

SONJA: Pick it up yourself.

REMI: Now who's being stupid?

SONJA: Take your dummy out your mouth before you speak to me.

REMI: And what about the baby?

SONJA: The hand that rocks the cradle turns the world and it's a woman's hand. Go finish your studies.

REMI: I love you and I'm going to marry you.

SONJA: I don't think you will, Remi. I haven't been for a walk but I've had a long train journey and I've done some thinking of my own. For a start, if you were really interested in me you'd have realized how important it is for me, an orphan girl, to be about to become a mother and getting married and all that, and you'd understand how important it was for me to stay with that pathetic little suitcase tonight and miss the party. But you don't, do you? And you don't really care at all otherwise you'd want to talk to your father. That's the real problem, isn't it? Why he's leaving and why you're letting him order you about. Why you're not communicating or at least just telling him to fuck off.

REMI: I do want to talk to him and he's not ordering me about.

SONJA: And?

(Pause.)

REMI: He's leaving because it's driving him mad. He isn't really getting anywhere. She puts it all down to 'headaches'.

(Pause.)

He can't bend over much further in order to get a promotion or else he'll fall flat on his face. *(Pause.)*

He can't face failure.

SONJA: What failure?

REMI: Spiritual failure… I think.

SONJA: Remi, all that's just romantic rubbish. Don't you see that if he actually does go, the real failure he is going to face is out there because nothing will have changed. That's the tragedy of the immigrant. They change faster than the countries they have left behind and they can never go back and be happy. Yet they can't be happy in their adopted countries because it's not home. Don't you see? You've spent too much time with your head in books, Remi. You're still making excuses for him. Jesus Christ, what's he ever done for you? What about your mother? Does he love you? Does she love you?

REMI: I don't know. I was brought up by a succession of different women, all of whom blurred into each other. I'm not sure which was my mother.

Probably none of them. Sick, isn't it?

(Pause.)

SONJA: Remi, if you don't know that then he's not just given you nothing in terms of talking to you, he's half-destroyed you before you've even had a chance to live. He can't love you. He can't even like you.

REMI: He likes me enough to want me to finish my degree and not to marry you, even for a baby.

SONJA: You don't have to marry me. Especially not now I've actually come to where you live and seen how you behave. You and her, you're both victims of lies and more lies. You've no desire to find anything out over and above what'll keep your head above water.

REMI: But I want to marry you, I know that. Do you think that's just keeping my head above water?

SONJA: Jesus!

REMI: *(Picking up the ring.)* Take it back.

SONJA: No.

(REMI is left holding the ring, RUTH comes out through the conservatory.)

RUTH: I can't sleep for worrying about your father.

REMI: I'm going out to find him.

RUTH: *(Nervously.)* Do you want your jacket?

REMI: No.

(To SONJA.)

I won't be long.

(He goes off. RUTH goes back to the conservatory to switch off the fairy lights. She comes back out.)

RUTH: It'll soon be morning.

SONJA: I'm sorry.

(Pause.)

For being such a bitch.

RUTH: It's late. Can I get you anything?

SONJA: *(Getting up.)* I'll get myself a glass of water...

(She doesn't know what to call RUTH.)

RUTH: Ruth.

SONJA: Ruth. Then I'll wait.

(She goes to move off and then stops and turns round and looks at RUTH.)

They say a son brought up by a mother grows up stronger but that's probably because secretly he grows to hate his father for not being there.

(Looking at her stomach.) What do you think?

RUTH: I don't know.

(Pause.)

SONJA: Have you got any family?

RUTH: I used to have…before I…

SONJA: I see. I didn't realize it could be that simple. I'm sorry.

RUTH: Funny thing is, I don't think I am. I'm better off without them.

(Pause.)

In some ways, if you really love somebody, if you really want something, then families aren't all that important. That's what I think.

Thought.

SONJA: I see.

(Pause.)

RUTH: Somebody once said that they'd always depended on the kindness of strangers. Well, that's me since I've been married.

SONJA: But you're not that weak.

RUTH: Like everybody, though, I could be if I wasn't careful.

(Pause.)

SONJA: I used to think I was lonely living in an orphanage, but I don't think I've ever met anyone as lonely as you, though. *(Pause.)*

You don't fit into the plan at all, do you?

RUTH: *(Smiling weakly.)* It's late. I think you'd better get your drink of water. There are glasses by the tap in the kitchen.

(SONJA goes off. RUTH goes back in the conservatory and turns on the fairy lights again. She comes back out, then returns, turns off the lights and goes off.)

(Lights change downstage and ALBERT enters with a suitcase. He begins packing frantically.)

MURIEL: *(Offstage.)* I made some sweetcorn for you.

ALBERT: No time.

(MURIEL enters.)

MURIEL: You going out again…at this time of night? What about Remi?

ALBERT: What the fuck you talking about Remi for? I going out by myself.

MURIEL: Has something happened?

ALBERT: Stop talking in my ears and lemme get on with my packing.

(He goes off to get some more clothes. Offstage REMI begins to cry.)

MURIEL: *(Defensively.)* Sometimes you look at us as if you hate us.

ALBERT: Shut up!

(Offstage REMI cries out 'Mummy'. VINCE enters.)

MURIEL: Hush, Remi. Vince?

186

VINCE: Albert here?

(He hesitates. MURIEL also hesitates for a moment.)

MURIEL: Well…

(ALBERT steps out and continues to pack. VINCE comes into the room.)

VINCE: What you think the plan is now, Albert?

ALBERT: Is you the one who knows all about England.

MURIEL: What happen?

ALBERT: Is a problem I think you better solve.

MURIEL: For Christ's sake, what happen?

VINCE: Albert?

ALBERT: Club burn down. Somebody paint, 'Fuck off niggers' on the walls and throw petrol down the steps and set fire to it.

MURIEL: Oh my God!

ALBERT: Is a risk you take with investment in this fucking country.

MURIEL: Jesus Christ.

VINCE: Albert, the place upstairs is burned out too.

ALBERT: You fucking stupid or what! All we own is the basement.

VINCE: It's not as simple as that.

ALBERT: Bollocks.

MURIEL: All the money gone?

ALBERT: Shut up! I don't know what you want to do with it anyway. House is no good for you. This room is big enough for you and the child.

MURIEL: What you mean, me and the child?

ALBERT: Well, I can't stay around at the moment. Things is too hot.

VINCE: You can't stay around?

MURIEL: What do you mean?

VINCE: Boy, you better...

ALBERT: Don't fucking 'boy' me, old man. Is you who tell me this country is too tough for some, is you who warn me to protect myself as a black man, and I done so. Remember when we decide not to bother with drinks licence or burglary and fire insurance. Remember! *(He shouts and REMI starts crying again.)*

VINCE: I remember.

ALBERT: Well I put the fucking club in your name.

VINCE: You did what?

ALBERT: You want me to say it again?

MURIEL: Albert?

(ALBERT has finished his packing now.)

ALBERT: *(To MURIEL.)* I going send some money for the child. You try and take him out the country and I come after you and break every bone in your fucking body!

(To VINCE.) I hope it turn out fine but is unfortunate I can't be there to help you.

VINCE: You leaving me?

ALBERT: So what happen? Is two wives I have in this room or what? I come here to work not live, and when I done work till I can't do so no more is now I going leave this backside place. I don't be like you, Vince. I can't sit here and listen to me arteries hardening and life passing me by. Boy, this place so fucking cold you can see your own breath escaping from your body and I sure one day I going breathe out and there don't going be any left. And what happen then, you think any white man going spill tears for me? White man here can brush him teeth and kill a black man at the same time but you all don't see it yet. All black man in this country wants is a uniform, British Rail, London Transport, Traffic Warden, R.A.F., any fucking thing, a uniform and a big stick.

(He points at VINCE.)

Is you who tell me England is not a place for a dreamer, but while you dreaming I is scheming. Survival at all costs. England. A country in which if a person have a little sickness in the head they send people to come lock them up like they is criminal. A country in which when you starts to get old your own family cart you off to some 'home' or something, like you is a horse. You think I going let that happen to me? You think I don't know how to play this system and win? I go check you later.

(ALBERT pushes past him and leaves. VINCE looks staggered. MURIEL helps him to sit down and gives him a glass of water. She sees the tears in his eyes. He makes no attempt to wipe them away. She stands over VINCE. Offstage REMI starts to cry again.)

MURIEL: What's going to happen, Vince?

VINCE: I don't know. Are you going to be all right?

MURIEL: We haven't got much choice, have we?

VINCE: What happened to him?

(Offstage REMI cries out 'Mummy'.)

MURIEL: Hush, Remi. Hush up now.

VINCE: What happened?

(Blackout.)

(We hear the sound of a ship's hooter and activity at the docks. The lights brighten to Caribbean moonlight. Enter ALBERT carrying the suitcase that we saw in Act One when they arrived. He is slightly out of breath. MURIEL holds REMI. She stands next to HUSTON.)

ALBERT: The man say the ship ready to go.

HUSTON: It sound like it… *(He looks at his watch.)* Is nearly midnight. *(Pause.)*

I just see the O'Connell boy getting on. I never did see anyone with so many books.

ALBERT: He hoping to study law.

HUSTON: So I hear.

(Pause.)

ALBERT: I think I better take the case and secure a place on the boat.

HUSTON: I suppose you better.

(Pause. ALBERT picks up the case then puts it down. He extends his hand which HUSTON takes.)

ALBERT: I don't have no trade but I going do my best to look after she and the child when we gets to England.

HUSTON: I hope so.

(ALBERT looks at MURIEL, who is looking at REMI.)

ALBERT: I will.

(To MURIEL.)

Don't leave it too late, Muriel.

(She smiles in reply.)

HUSTON: She won't.

(ALBERT picks up the case and leaves for the boat.) You all right?

(MURIEL nods.)

You don't want to go? *(No answer.)*

Give it a try for your son's sake. You have your mother's money. Put down the money on some property. Yes?

(MURIEL nods.)

MURIEL: Will you write?

HUSTON: Every week as long as I have strength in my body.

(MURIEL goes to her father, who hugs her. He takes the baby from her and holds him up above his head. The ship's hooter goes again.) *(To REMI.)*

A new land, Remi.

(The hooter goes again.) A new land.

MURIEL: *(Taking REMI.)* Goodbye father.

(MURIEL kisses him and goes off to the ship. He can't say anything. He stands there then waves reflectively. The hooter goes for the last time. He waves at her with a new vigour.)

HUSTON: So long!

(He waves like mad then he stops. Nothing. It is silent. The sense of something having ended abounds.)

(REMI comes through into the garden and peers into the darkness. He can't see anything but he senses there is something happening.)

HUSTON: *(Softly.)* Remi Huston Williams. You all better look after that boy.

(REMI begins to walk down the garden toward HUSTON, who exits. Pause. SONJA comes out through the conservatory.)

SONJA: Remi?

(REMI turns.)

REMI: You were asleep.

(He begins to come toward her.)

SONJA: I know. It's been a long day.

REMI: Sorry. All right?

SONJA: Stomach feels a bit funny but I know why that is.

REMI: Where is she?

SONJA: She said she's gone to lie down and think for an hour or so. She's probably got a lot to think about. *(Pause.)*

Why don't you like her?

REMI: She's just another of the women. Because he married this one means nothing to me.

SONJA: She's not as bad as you think…

(Pause.)

In fact I quite like her.

REMI: I'm happy for you.

(Pause.)

SONJA: Did you see your father?

REMI: I found him singing on one of the bridges by the river. Tommy Steele songs. He kept trying to give me that toothy grin. I nearly threw up.

SONJA: What's the matter with him? Was he drunk?

REMI: Sick. Kept telling me his life began when he stepped down the stairs of the plane and kissed the tarmac at Heathrow.

SONJA: Didn't you come here by boat?

REMI: I don't know.

(Pause.)

SONJA: Where is he?

REMI: He'll be here in a minute. I left him at the corner of the street. He said he wanted to make a dignified entrance and not have to be seen to be escorted home by his son.

(Pause.)

SONJA: I've been thinking. I'm going to ask him why I'm not good enough for you.

REMI: Why? He's screwed up as it is. Can't you just let him go and forget it? We can do what we like after he's gone.

SONJA: Forget it! Do you think I could marry you without knowing that he cares? I'll let him go but I want him to say he's pleased or something, to my face. I don't think that's asking too much, do you?

(Pause.)

Unless he's got a thing about black women.

REMI: Don't be stupid. My mother was black.

SONJA: These days there's a lot of black mothers but not a lot of black wives.

REMI: It's nothing to do with it.

SONJA: Remi, I don't want any more fear and doubt. I want this child, our baby, to inherit a stable and well-ordered past. Something he or she can make into a platform for the future. Already it's only got a quarter of the grandparents it should have, and if that one don't want to know then it's better off just living with me because I know what will happen. You'll just end up running back to your father and I've no desire to be east to his west, the north to his south. I think we, the three of us, will have enough problems without that.

REMI: You don't trust me?

SONJA: It's him I don't trust. I've met him through you, Remi.

(Pause.)

REMI: Sonja, just let him go in one piece. Let him piss off and we'll forget him.

SONJA: No Remi, you won't forget him. You see, you love him too much. You're going to have to face up to him now or not at all.

REMI: Don't you think I've tried?

SONJA: Try again, try harder.

(Enter RUTH. She has obviously just woken up.)

RUTH: Is Albert back?

REMI: He'll be back in a minute.

(Pause.)

He's all right. He just went for a walk. He hasn't slit
his wrists or anything. *(He looks hard at her.)* What's the
matter?

RUTH: Nothing.

SONJA: Have you finished packing?

RUTH: Almost.

REMI: Who turned off the lights? He'll want them on.

RUTH: I forgot.

*(REMI goes to switch them back on again. RUTH sits beside SONJA.
She pulls her dressing gown close.)*

SONJA: Was it a good party?

RUTH: Quiet, but nice.

(Pause.)

SONJA: Can I ask you something?

RUTH: I'm not sure if I'll be able to answer. I'm not very good
at conversations.

SONJA: Were you married before?

RUTH: No. On the shelf till I was twenty-three.

SONJA: How old are you now?

RUTH: Thirty-two.

(The lights come on.)

SONJA: It's warm tonight.

RUTH: When I was a girl I used to spend the summers with my
parents at their villa in Greece. Every night was like this.
Warm, still, bright, serene. All we need now is the crickets.
Little choirs of them. First one group, then the next, then

altogether. I'd always fall asleep and daddy would pick me up and carry me in. Till he got too old to bend.

SONJA: Did you go to school there?

RUTH: Boarding school, Surrey. Then secretarial college in Oxford.

SONJA: Then marriage?

RUTH: Then mummy and daddy died, then marriage. Predictable.

(Pause.)

SONJA: You're not very happy, are you?

RUTH: We were.

SONJA: But what about you?

(No answer from RUTH. Re-enter REMI.)

REMI: He's coming in.

ALBERT: *(Offstage.)* Anybody at home or you all gone home without me?

RUTH: Is he all right?

REMI: *(Snapping.)* How am I supposed to know?

SONJA: Remi!

(Enter ALBERT looking energetic and pleased.)

ALBERT: What, another party so soon?

REMI: This is Sonja.

ALBERT: So, you arrive at last. Pleased to meet you.

(He kisses her hand and winks.)

I met a few Sonja's in me time. Ruth, you give the girl
a drink?

RUTH: Yes.

ALBERT: Well, what about the rest of us, then?

(To them all.)

Well, come on and party it up a little; don't be shy. Son,
what you want?

REMI: Nothing thanks.

ALBERT: Sonja? You see, I remember. I got a good memory
when I put me mind to it.

SONJA: I'm all right, thank you.

RUTH: Can I get you anything, Albert?

ALBERT: Well, not now, in front of the children.

(He laughs: to SONJA.)

I understand you having a baby and you want to marry
my son. Take him out of University.

SONJA: I'm having his baby, we want to marry, and he wants
to leave University.

ALBERT: You think you come clever too, nuh, but I been
around a long time. I know your game.

RUTH: Albert, please.

(She comes up close to him.)

ALBERT: *(To SONJA.)* I one step ahead of you.

(RUTH goes to ALBERT and gently takes his arm.)

RUTH: Please, Albert.

197

(ALBERT pushes RUTH away from him with the flat of his hand against her face. RUTH stumbles and falls.)

ALBERT: Why you don't just fuck off out me face, cow.

(SONJA goes to RUTH and helps her get up. RUTH is hurt and bruised. She is crying. She hurries away into the dining room and off.)

REMI: You don't have to talk to her that way.

ALBERT: Talk to who what way?

REMI: Either of them.

ALBERT: Oh, I see. You come a man again. This time in front of your woman.

SONJA: I'm not just his woman.

ALBERT: What, you mean you everybody's woman? I tell you she type is no good for you, boy. If she work hard she might come a typist or work at McDonald's or do some other black woman's job.

SONJA: Fuck off!

REMI: Sonja!

SONJA: Sonja what! You think I'm going to listen to some drunken old black man calling me a whore and telling me that I can either sit behind some man's desk or serve Big Macs all my life?

REMI: He's my father.

SONJA: Well, you can keep him.

ALBERT: Son, this is the woman you want to marry?

(He laughs out loudly.)

She curse like a white man.

REMI: She has every right to swear after what you've just done and said. I don't care what you say any longer. I'm just going to do what I want to do because I'm sick! Sick! Sick of you messing up my life!

SONJA: *(To REMI.)* And you think it's just your life he's messing up.

(To ALBERT.)

I've never heard of anyone as selfish as you. You're like all black men, think the world owes them a favour so they can behave how they like, whether it's throwing bottles and bricks at the police or smashing women in the face.

ALBERT: Why you don't just fuck off out me house, thinking you can come in here and accuse me of this and that and all kinds of other frigging nonsense. So go on and fuck off, and take your ugly little foetus with you. I going get a drink.

(He takes the empty bottle and goes off for another drink. Pause while SONJA calms down.)

REMI: I'm sorry.

SONJA: It's sick.

REMI: What is?

SONJA: You! You just stand there and listen to that lunacy and say nothing. Sick!

REMI: I did say something. What else do you want me to say? 'Dad, I don't think you should talk to her like that', or 'Dad, this is the woman I'm going to marry, so please...'

SONJA: Woman you're going to marry!

(REMI digs in his pocket.)

REMI: The ring's here, I want you to take it.

SONJA: Remi.

REMI: Take it!

SONJA: No.

REMI: Why?

SONJA: No, because I want my ugly little foetus to have a big beautiful mature life. Before you bring either me or a child into your life I think you should make up your mind about your father. You'd better talk to him, and fast.

REMI: I'll talk to him.

SONJA: *(Standing up.)* Well, phone me when you do.

REMI: Please stay, Sonja.

SONJA: I said, phone me when you find out.

(She moves to go out then stops.)

If it's any consolation, I still love you, Remi. But for me it isn't everything. Like most wasted children I'm used to living without it. But it'll be different for my child. No man who can call an innocent unborn child an ugly little foetus is really capable of love. Bye Remi.

(She goes. REMI looks at the ring and slips it into his pocket. He waits. He is determined now. After a moment or two ALBERT comes in. He switches off the fairy lights.)

ALBERT: She gone?

REMI: Yes.

ALBERT: Women who give you lip just deserve a slap. You should have slapped she in the mouth.

REMI: What good would that have done?

ALBERT: When I first come to this country white woman do anything for a piece of black man and is true today...

REMI: *(Almost stammering.)* I want you to say you like her and that you don't mind us getting married.

ALBERT: ...though in a different way, I suppose. So how come you ends up with an ugly little black girl? I mean, I could have fixed you up with something better myself, from the stable, though they not as good as they used to be. But fine thoroughbred material. Me don't want no half-breeds, which is why I don't breed with she.

(He points off to the house where RUTH is.)

REMI: I'll finish my degree first but I want to marry her.

(Pause.)

I really do.

(ALBERT pauses then looks at him with great concentration.)

ALBERT: It's as if this country had opened her great mouth to welcome us, licked us, sucked on us a little, swallowed and passed us out via her bowels. Useless, brown, shapeless objects of waste. Have you ever looked closely at a lump of shit? They say inside every black man is a white man trying to get out. I say inside every lump of shit is a black man trying to get out.

(RUTH is seen in the dining room with a suitcase, scarf and coat. She is leaving him, and during the next few lines she leaves for good.

Before she goes she looks out unseen from the conservatory as he speaks. Then she goes, switching off the lights inside the house.)

REMI: Dad, please talk to me. I'm not a boy any more. It's not too late. I love Sonja. I'm proud. I'm nearly happy.

ALBERT: Jesus Christ, is soon going be morning and time to leave. Sunrise. Though most the time in England there don't be no fucking sun to rise. Is just dayrise and that don't be no good for the immigrant.

REMI: Well then, tell me why you're going. Talk to me!

ALBERT: 'I noticed the medal.' 'Is nothing really. Everyone who finish get one.' 'Back home a medal like that make you famous.' 'But it can't buy me food. England going teach you practicalities.'

REMI: What?

ALBERT: 'Don't fucking "boy" me, old man. Is you who tell me this country too tough for some.'

REMI: I didn't say anything.

ALBERT: But Vincent, prison don't be such a bad place. At least it take you away from the pressure. *(Pause.)* Hah!

REMI: Dad?

ALBERT: Hush, Remi. Listen.

(MURIEL appears on stage. She walks into the spotlight.)

MURIEL: Dear Albert, I've left Remi in a children's home. The address is on the back of the envelope. He's still young so he need never know anything about it, or about me, if you don't want. His future is up to you. I can't afford to take him back with me. It's not the money so much as the fact that I am not strong enough.

ALBERT: Listen to your mother.

(REMI is mystified and frightened. During the following speech he runs into the house and shouts 'Ruth' then comes back out. She is not there. He realizes she has left.)

MURIEL: I love you still but you have learnt how to destroy. You is too good at destroying and I have no confidence left when you are around. I tried to go out to church with Remi to pray but the vicar just smile and say, 'Nice to see you but don't come back again.' Back home vicar is vocation not job, but here I see vicar going down the pub and it makes me want to cry. I knew England would be like this but I couldn't tell my father even though I wanted to.

(Pause.)

Well, now he dead so I going home. I doubt if you will ever leave England so I won't see you again because I'm not coming back. I hope you get what you want. Muriel.

(MURIEL stays there and holds the letter.)

ALBERT: She don't know a damn thing.

REMI: Who doesn't? Who are you talking about?

ALBERT: Hush up. You can't see she there?

(ALBERT points toward MURIEL but REMI sees nothing. From the other side of the stage LYNN comes on. She is visibly pregnant and tatty. She walks into the spotlight.)

LYNN: Albert.

(He spins round.)

ALBERT: Well, say what you got to say, then.

LYNN: I was going to write but I'm not too good at it. I'm sorry to have to come down here in front of all your friends.

ALBERT: Well, speak up, nuh.

REMI: I didn't say anything.

LYNN: I don't want you to marry me but I need money.

ALBERT: Money for what?

LYNN: You know what. The baby.

ALBERT: Just fuck off!

(Sounds of male laughter.)

LYNN: Just what?

(Echo of 'just what' and LYNN freezes. Cross-fade sound and light to MURIEL.)

MURIEL: P.S. I would like for you to give Remi my address when he gets old enough to write to me. I hope you will find it in your heart to do this. *(MURIEL goes off.)*

LYNN: You've got to help me, Albert.

ALBERT: You just open your mouth again and the next time you do so going be in the dentist chair.

(To REMI.) You have your mother's address?

REMI: Whose?

ALBERT: Your mother, Muriel's.

(LYNN gathers strength. ALBERT is ignoring her.)

LYNN: I loved you, Albert.

(She spits. Silence all round. ALBERT wipes his face with his sleeve. LYNN leaves.)

ALBERT: They've gone.

REMI: Talk to me!

ALBERT: A wedding. My son. To a black girl. In England.

REMI: Sonja.

ALBERT: Is morning and I have to go and pick me mango.

REMI: Dad, what's the matter?

ALBERT: Son, I love you too much. I want you to succeed too much. I going gather some mango. Soon be rainy season.

REMI: Dad?

ALBERT: A traveller is a man of knowledge. You hear the sea? Maybe I go for a swim first. *(He begins to take off his clothes down to his trousers.)*

Is good to be back home and have to make these little decisions. First mango or swimming? Son, you just watch me clothes like a man. *(He starts walking down the garden.)*

REMI: Dad, please. I don't understand. I'm frightened.

ALBERT: At last you realize you is in England. Is not a simple place like back home.

(Pause.)

If I don't come back you can keep the clothes.

(He goes off.)

END OF PLAY

THE SHELTER

'Remember a shelter is a temporary place of refuge in a disaster. It cannot be like home.'

A message from UNDRO – Pan Caribbean Disaster Preparedness And Prevention Project. St. John's, Antigua.

(Sign on the wall of the Ministry of Education, Health and Social Affairs. St. Kitts.)

Act One

HER

About thirty-five. A country lady from
somewhere between Bath and Bristol

HIM

About forty-five. He looks a challenging man

Notes

This act is set sometime towards the end of the
eighteenth century, the age of the Augustans,
of all that is rational and exact.

The music for HER song in Act One is
Haydn's *Symphony No. 39* in G Minor (second
movement), and this can also be used as
incidental music at both the start and the end
of Act One.

Act One

The lights come up on a stretch of white sand. On this beach are two sloping palms, some seaweed, some pieces of wood, a few coconuts, some masting, and some coconut shells.

The sun is high and we can hear the sea.

Downstage there is a woman lying on the sand. She is asleep, or unconscious, but clearly not dead for she stirs slightly. Then she is quiet again. She has on a tatty, long dress, but her legs are bare and she has on only the one shoe.

A man enters. He has on a large white cotton shirt, knee breeches, but no stockings or shoes. His hair is rough and full of sand and his face is slightly cut and scarred. Into the top of his breeches he has tucked a small knife. He carries a bundle of pieces of wood of different sizes which he piles down beside those that are already there. He looks at the woman and takes off his shirt. He places it over the woman to shield her from the sun. He moves offstage again.

After a few seconds the man comes back on with more wood. He goes across and stands over the woman as if checking to make sure that she is still breathing. She stirs and he drops back.

Overhead a gull cackles. The man looks up and accidentally drops the wood. He turns back to see the woman pulling herself up and looking at him.

HER: Do not touch me. I mean you no harm.

> *(She moves backwards, throwing his shirt off her. She holds on to the foot of a palm tree.)*

HIM: There is nothing to fear.

HER: Do not approach me.

HIM: I promise you, I have no desire to harm you.

(He carefully picks up his shirt and puts it on.)

I sought to protect you from the heat of the sun with this, my shirt.

HER: You speak English?

HIM: I do. It is my only language.

(Pause.)

HER: Is this your country?

HIM: Like you I was of England, whose chalk-cliffed fringes we may never again set our eyes upon. *(Pause.)*

HER: Where are we?

HIM: I cannot be sure.

(Pause.)

HER: Do not come any closer.

HIM: I bear you no malice.

HER: Remain where you are. *(Pause. She looks around.)* Who are you?

HIM: My name or my position?

HER: What are you?

HIM: I am nobody to you.

(Pause.)

I have things to do.

(He turns and goes offstage. She runs a nervous hand through her hair and tries to take stock of her surroundings. He comes back in with another bundle of wood and drops it.)

HER: How do we come to be here? Are there no others?

HIM: The ship splintered and cast us both asunder.

HER: We two alone?

HIM: I assume the others to have perished.

(Pause.)

It would appear our situation is the matter from which books are written, fortunes made.

(He continues to pile up the wood and shred the various materials into binding.)

HER: You have markings of some sort upon your face.

(He reaches up and wipes away the dirt, etc.)

HIM: Bruising from the wreckage. I bled profusely.

(Pause.)

HER: Tell me truly how I come to find myself on these shores. I am near three decades adrift from childhood.

HIM: I discovered you clinging to a length of planking and I hauled you onto this sand.

HER: You rescued me?

HIM: It may be more accurate to intimate that I certainly prevented your drowning.

(Pause.)

At first I thought your death an inescapable certainty. For the last two days you have lain between heaven and earth.

HER: And what did you do with me?

HIM: Gave you water, what little fruit you could eat. I tried not to move your person beyond what was strictly necessary.

HER: You touched me?

HIM: I dragged you bodily from the ocean.

HER: I wish to sit upright. *(He moves towards her.)* I need no assistance.

(Pause.)

I have no recollection of your being aboard the ship. What was your position?

HIM: Merely a voyager.

HER: Of what status?

HIM: A common status.

(Pause. He continues binding the wood.)

HER: And what of our geography? You must have some notion of our position. Is this Africa?

HIM: If you look back to the hills...

(He points.)

You may have to stand to see them.

HER: I need not instruction in how to observe.

HIM: From their summit it is possible for one to observe the whole island and beyond. There is nothing but sea in every direction.

HER: Then this is an island?

HIM: It is.

HER: The mist and cloud must obscure the horizon.

HIM: The days have been clear.

(Pause.)

HER: And what of the population of this so-called island?

HIM: We would appear to constitute the population.

HER: You are my sole companion?

HIM: I am.

HER: I do not believe you. Your understanding is weak.

HIM: It is based on exploration. Knowledge.

(Pause.)

HER: You masquerade as a gentleman. What are you?

HIM: A man. Gentle by nature.

HER: I have no desire to talk with you. I feel sure you have not within you the capacity for reason.

(They stare at each other, then he again begins to line up the wood into different lengths and bind it together. She pretends to be concerned with her dress and wiping clean her bruises and the dirt from off her face. She tries to untangle her hair. He wipes his brow then goes for more wood. He comes back and once again begins the whole process of binding and sorting.)

Do you not feel ashamed to look at me in that manner?

HIM: I know not what manner it is you speak of.

HER: That unclean manner.

HIM: I have not looked upon you in any manner, clean or unclean. I am occupied.

HER: To what possible end?

HIM: Constructing an ungainly but secure refuge from wrappings of cloth and strands of foliage.

HER: I trust you are not thinking I might be encouraged to enter into it with something such as yourself.

HIM: I understand.

HER: You must possess fanciful notions of my character.

HIM: Our acquaintance has been too brief for such speculation.

HER: A theatrical thing such as yourself conversing with ceremony?

HIM: I am not offended that you do not wish to share my island chambers.

HER: It would be akin to breaking bread with the devil.

(Pause.)

HIM: I know not why it is you wish to fight with me.

(Pause. He continues with what he was doing.)

HER: Why do you choose to construct a dwelling?

HIM: To avoid death from the naked heat of the sun and its resultant giddiness. And, if there be wild animals loose on the island we must have need of some defences to preserve our lives.

HER: Wild animals?

HIM: Hypothesis is near cousin to safety with knowledge as scant as our own.

HER: There are no wild animals. Either your imagination is defective or your exploration superficial.

(He carries on with what he is doing and again he goes off for more wood. He brings it back on and gets to the next stage in the construction of his shelter. She 'bravely' stands and looks about herself. She takes off her one shoe and takes something out of it. She wipes it clean on her sleeve and puts it back on. She begins to take an interest in what he is doing but she does not want him to see she is interested.)

Is it your idleness of race prevents your building a boat?

(Pause. He ignores her.)

And tell me, are you truly bereft of human faculties?

HIM: I am not possessed of the skills necessary to construct a boat.

(Pause. She walks about a little.)

HER: I shall not be staying here. We cannot be far from the African mainland and we can sail there swiftly.

HIM: Have you some knowledge of which direction to set sail?

HER: It is quite straightforward. You will read the stars.

HIM: It is the middle of the afternoon.

HER: You overestimate your cleverness, ape.

(Pause.)

HIM: I shall continue in the construction of quarters, for night will be upon us sooner than we may imagine.

HER: And tomorrow?

HIM: I shall arise and approach the day with both care and caution.

HER: No, you will build a boat.

HIM: And what of the weather? We two alone survive a storm that sank an ocean-going vessel.

HER: The storm has blown over.

HIM: But there will be others to follow. And what of supplies? Fresh water? Food-stocks?

HER: We shall manage.

(Pause. He picks up two of the coconut shells.)

HIM: I have found inland a freshwater stream. Do you wish to explore?

HER: I shall go nowhere, heathen.

(He goes off and she waits a moment before coming over and looking at the wood and binding, etc. She picks up a stick but throws it down in disgust. She turns and looks out to sea. He comes back in, carrying more binding.)

HIM: I have noticed you have on only the one shoe.

HER: It is no concern of yours.

HIM: Why not remove it and walk barefoot in comfort?

HER: I was not born of savage stock.

(Pause. She looks at him but he continues to work.)

HIM: What might a lady such as yourself be doing aboard the *St. Christopher*?

HER: Nothing that would concern something of your kind.

HIM: Perhaps not.

(Pause.)

I assume your husband to be a merchant on the coast.

HER: He will certainly set sail to search me out.

HIM: Then it would appear there is no reason for us to risk our lives upon uncharted seas.

HER: You will construct a boat.

HIM: But there is much to eat. We might cook on alternate days.

HER: Cook?

HIM: Seagulls' eggs, fish, crab, fruit.

HER: Impudent.

(Pause. She turns away from him. He starts to dig out the sand so that he can erect the walls.) I command you to build me a means of leaving these shores.

HIM: There is nothing here to make you important to me, nothing that might induce me to obey the harshness of your voice. *(Pause.)*

HER: I know you as an escaped slave, do I not?

(He laughs.)

HIM: A slave, lady? Where are my chains? Where is my master? Are you my mistress? *(Pause. He continues to laugh.)* How am I a slave?

HER: Nigger.

HIM: Lady, I am a free man in as much as any man is able to be free. I belong to nobody.

HER: You remain here out of fear of what might befall you if you leave, slave.

HIM: I remain because I choose to remain.

(He carries on building and she looks at the sea.)

HER: Do you have a name, slave?

221

HIM: They tell me it is Thomas Samuels.

HER: Who are 'they'?

HIM: Your family, lady.

HER: You do not know of my family.

HIM: And you do not know of mine, lady.

HER: Your family attachments are those of a dog.

(Pause.)

You may call me Mrs. Darnley or Ma'am. I am not accustomed to being addressed as 'lady'. *(He laughs.)*

I find your laughter primitive.

(Pause.)

Your lips are uncommonly thick. Can you say, 'Ma'am'?

HIM: Ma'am.

HER: You surprise me.

(Pause.)

If we must pass some minutes here it is only Christian to name the island.

(Pause.)

'Palm Tree Island' would seem both accurate and relevant.

HIM: I have already named it 'The Island'.

HER: 'The Island'? You mean to give it no name at all?

HIM: It is accurate. It betrays nothing.

(She laughs.)

HER: It is stupid. Uncivilized. *(Pause.)*

When you have completed your games you will light a fire to attract the attention of passing ships.

HIM: It would involve one of us living on top of the hill to keep it ablaze, for it is the only true vantage point.

HER: Then you must live there.

(He ignores her and strains to support and put up some of the shelter. He does so, making a very flimsy hut. He stands back from it, having tossed the knife down by the excess binding.)

It is truly grotesque. I would expect little more from you.

(He picks up a bit of stick and begins to draw idly in the sand.)

(Looking at the shelter.) I quite fail to see the other room.

(He looks angrily at her.)

My sleeping quarters.

HIM: You sleep where you stand.

HER: You need a stiff beating, Samuels. You have no manners in the presence of a lady.

HIM: It matters little to me be you a lady or a vagabond.

HER: And you claim you are free, that you have nothing to fear from the company of other men.

HIM: I have much to fear in any man's presence but it is not the chains that I dread, it is the manner of thought that flashes between a man's clapping eyes on me and the opening of his mouth. It is not his touch but the hesitation before his touch. In England I was nothing, a man of colour labouring for a nobleman, born into servitude, for England is too perfumed a country to soil her own people with the word slavery.

(Pause.)

But some masters die, and mine did oblige. *(Pause.)*

And what in this Africa that we set sail for? Will you and your husband try and buy this freeman as your slave?

(Pause.)

Though I be no man's slave, lady, I remain a slave to the state of your world, but I fear you not. I may yet find a corner of this earth where you do not exist.

(She walks away from him.)

HER: Construct a boat and take me but a part of the way. You may cut me loose in a smaller boat and thereafter roam where you will. *(Pause.)*

I have money. I will pay you.

(She reaches down into the pockets of her dress and pulls loose a couple of coins. He begins to draw in the sand.)

HIM: I do not wish to leave our island.

HER: I am no part of it. Is there no talking to you?

HIM: I know not how to construct a boat.

(Pause.)

And I see not a wedding ring upon your finger.

(She stares at him for a long while, then she runs and picks up the knife, which is on the sand. She turns to face him.)

HER: You will build a boat and take me away.

HIM: Woman, your words betray foolishness.

HER: No, slave. I am sincere in my convictions. Do not come any closer.

HIM: And to where shall we sail?

HER: Navigation is a skill more becoming a man.

HIM: And am I now a man?

(Pause.)

Lady, I do not see your overseer. Does a knife alone now give you authority over me? *(He takes a step towards her.)*

HER: Do not come any closer or I shall do it.

HIM: Do what, lady?

(He takes the knife from her.)

We left behind such behaviour when I hauled you ashore.

HER: I cannot stay here with an ape.

(Pause.)

HIM: Then one of us must leave.

HER: Ape.

(Pause.)

HIM: Your ignorance clings to you like sand to a moist limb.

(They stare at each other; overhead a gull cackles. The sea is heard sliding up the beach and then it is quiet. He moves away from her and looks out to sea. She stares at him.)

SCENE TWO

Only a few moments have passed. She is sitting now. He looks at the shelter, then pushes at it and knocks it over. He stares at her, wanting to see her response. She drops her eyes and he goes offstage.

At first she does nothing but look out to sea. However, after a while she begins to worry if he is going to come back. She stands and moves nervously to where he went off, then she comes back and looks at the broken shelter.

Then she hears him and it startles her. She manages to sit down before he appears. He has his arms full of palm leaves. He throws them down and begins to arrange them. They say nothing to each other.

HER: You have been quite some time.

    (Pause. He ignores her.)

I dislike being left alone. Desertion is not mannerly.

    (He starts to work, unstripping some of the binding and reworking some of the rest. She watches him.) Tell me, why destroy your own construction? It seems uncommonly self-defeating.

    (Pause.)

I can only assume maritime matters are under way.

HIM: Perhaps you have spoken sufficiently as it is.

HER: I am not in need of your help in the conducting of my conversational affairs.

    (Pause.)

I should like to know if you are engaged in the process of building a vessel.

HIM: I am.

HER: And of what variety is this vessel?

HIM: A raft. It is the best I can do.

(She laughs.)

HER: You do not surprise me.

(Pause. He ignores her and continues working.)

I have no intention of reinforcing your own position,
do you understand?

(Pause.)

Merely remember you are in the presence of a lady who
has never before left England.

HIM: It would seem to matter not where you people go.
Your behaviour remains much the same.

(He draws a line in the sand with a piece of stick.)

I would rather you remained on the further side of
this line.

HER: And what is to happen if I venture to cross your line?

HIM: Perhaps nothing.

HER: You make little sense. You continue to converse as a child.

HIM: And you as someone who will continue to grow in
confidence and ignorance.

(Pause. She stands.)

HER: I intend to cross your line. Circumstances cannot alter
the clarity of the situation.

(He says nothing so she crosses the line.)

There. I have crossed it. What are your intentions?

HIM: They are simple. Upon the completion of this raft I shall take my departure.

HER: And what of me?

HIM: There is fresh water and food. You will survive.

HER: I must accompany you. To abandon me would be murder.

HIM: Lady, you belittle me.

HER: And you me with the staleness of your black mind.

(Pause.)

HIM: Your husband will find you.

HER: My husband is dead. A squire, thirty years older than I.

(Pause.)

I am a widow going to the coast in the hope of attracting a good match amongst the merchants there.

(Pause.)

I am not ashamed. My future husband will reward you handsomely.

HIM: Your future husband will be a trifle deaf, his ears affected by the bloodied screams of dying Africans. He will not know how to reward such as I.

HER: I will instruct him to let you have whatever it is you desire.

(He begins to laugh. She looks angrily to him.) Your fetid smell offends me.

(He continues to laugh until he is able to speak.)

HIM: I was born near two hundred years ago in a small
village in my native Africa.

(Pause.)

HER: Your statement lacks any proportion. It is that of a
nigger.

HIM: A village so small that I cannot remember the name
of it…and your father came and set fire to the hut of my
family, raped my mother and killed my own aged father,
but he did not kill me for I was young and strong. He
beat me till I bled unconscious on the ground. He chained
together my hands and my legs, then he fired an iron rod
and branded my skin as easily as a hot knife finds its way
through a waxen candle. The smell jolted my person to
consciousness.

(Pause.)

Then he placed me in a large ship with others of my
village and he took me to a country where he punished
me if I spoke my own language, to a country where he
whipped me if I worshipped my own Gods, and in their
place he gave me the cold European tongue I now speak
and the long-haired white man I am supposed to worship.

(Pause.)

When I had my children your father took them from me
as he took the grain that I had harvested, the cane that
I cut, the cotton that I picked, and he still takes them
from me.

I see your father in the face of every white man I discern,
and I do not want your future husband to reward me for
he has not the money to repay the debt.

HER: My father was a good man. He kept no niggers.

(He laughs.)

HIM: I am two hundred years old now, and getting older.
I wonder when you will die and we can begin anew?

HER: Do not threaten me.

HIM: Can you learn to perceive again? Witness the whole
red-stained world?

HER: I can see perfectly.

HIM: And what do you see?

HER: I see you. The awful thickness of your lips. Your tumid
nostrils, your teeth like small tusks, your eyes round and
mis-shapened like blackened farthings, your head covered
in a bestial fleece. I see that somebody has evidently
caused you a great hurt and you still smart with the pain;
you still try to achieve a primitive revenge.

HIM: I hurt for whosoever it was etched the first cut has never
troubled to dress the wound properly. And every time I
renew the dressing he comes and again he tears it off.

HER: I find your plea for pity sickening. Like all slaves you
merely beg.

HIM: I beg nothing from you.

(Pause. He turns away from her.) The light fails quickly.

(Pause.)

And we shall be in need of more wood for the fire.

*(She says nothing and he goes off. But he accidentally leaves behind
the knife. She bends down and picks it up. Then she tosses it back
down and waits... He comes back in and starts to construct a fire.
He feels in his waistband for the knife then realizes he has left it*

*behind. He looks down and he picks it up. She looks away. He starts
to cut up the bits of wood.)*

Tell me, why could you not find yourself a match in
England?

HER: It is not that simple. I have a position to maintain.

HIM: Order and degree.

HER: You may mock but it keeps our people above the animal,
gives us a purpose, and it is what is right in God's name.

HIM: It is you who are chained.

(Pause.)

Destined to echo the awful piety of a previous people.

HER: And what would you suggest?

HIM: Nothing. I know only that England has exchanged her
aristocracy for this new steam age, and her men of colour
will never be happy, will never dream without the sun
kissing their faces, till the cold morning strikes them alive.
And those amongst us, like you, who dare, must leave.
That is all I know. Nothing. There is no suggestion.

(Pause.)

HER: There must have been some desirable women of your
kind in England.

HIM: A few, but they too had positions to maintain. In the
kitchens of your family.

HER: And what of the lower English women? I hear that…

HIM: You see, I never before felt able to associate with
someone who, without the discipline of forethought,
merely realized of me as a nigger, or as a slave, or as one
who might take nourishment from eating the flesh of my

231

fellow human beings. I was always inclined towards the notion that I would, perhaps against my will, kill them.

(He stoops and strikes the knife against the stone. After a few attempts it catches fire on the dry sticks and moss, etc. He starts to blow on the fire to encourage it to flare up.) There. It is alight.

HER: You have some practical skills.

(Pause. He says nothing.)

It seems we have little choice but to pass this one night here.

HIM: We have everything we need. *(He tucks the knife into his belt.)* I shall gather more wood.

(He moves to go off.)

HER: No.

(He stops and turns to face her.)

The noises of the day seem magnified by night.

(Pause. He says nothing.)

If you wish to kill me, do so now and not whilst I sleep.

HIM: I shall not be long.

(She turns away and he throws down his knife without her seeing. Then he moves off quickly. She wanders nervously and sings quietly to herself. After a few minutes she begins to wonder where he is.)

HER: *(Singing.)* As it came on a bright day our Lord asked his mother,
If he might wander free, wander free, on the hill.
Up and down our sweet Lord ran till three poor young men,
Said to him come with us, come with us, you will see.

(She moves to where he has gone off and comes back to the fire where she sees the knife, which she picks up. She hovers over the fire, her

232

face glowing in the light. Gradually the silence of the night and the sound of the waves begin to take over. She is frightened and convinced that he has deserted her. She begins to sing again to keep herself company. Then out of the darkness he comes back.)

I was sure of your desertion.

HIM: I omitted to take my knife.

(He takes it from her and walks down past her to the edge of the sea.)

HER: I must admit to being fearful of the dark.

HIM: You were singing.

HER: It is no concern of yours.

HIM: It was possessed of a fine melody.

(Pause.)

HER: Are you not going for more wood?

HIM: I may manage with what I have.

(We hear the sea as they both wait in silence. Almost without knowing it she begins to sing to herself again.)

HER: *(Singing.)* Over fields ran he three poor men a chasing,
But a sight of such wealth, of such wealth, brought him
to his knee.
And fetched home Mary mild her child who suffered,
Then she took him into her arms, in her arms, and
affection showered she.

(He turns around and she stops abruptly.)

HIM: You sing well.

HER: I offer it more as a prayer than as a form of
entertainment. Something to help pass the night.

HIM: *(Quietly, as he moves away from her.)* And the next day, and the night, and the day after that.

(Pause. The noise of the sea grows angrier.)

HER: Did you choose to speak?

HIM: Only if you were listening, lady. Only if you chose to listen.

END OF ACT ONE

Act Two

Notes

This act is set in the bar of a pub in Ladbroke Grove, London, sometime in the 1950s.

Act Two

We are in a grimy Ladbroke Grove pub. It is mid-evening in mid-week and there are very few people in the bar.

IRENE: Close on thirty-five. She sits at a round, slightly unbalanced table by herself. She listens to the crackly jukebox as one fifties ballad finishes and the machinery heaves itself into another well-worn period tune. She is dressed in a skirt and top. She still has on a thin jacket, which we assume is too flimsy for the cold January weather outside. She clings to it and sips at her half pint of light ale. Her fingers and face are clean, though they look grubby and well-worn. Her face is pleasant, though tired, as she begins to slide into premature middle age. She is agitated and anxious.

Enter LOUIS: As if straight from work in his donkey jacket and working trousers and boots. He looks at IRENE for a moment then comes over, pint in hand, and stands over her. We see that his hands are chafed and dirty. He too looks tired.

IRENE looks up at LOUIS, then away from him, pretending to listen to the music, which eventually finishes.

Pause.

LOUIS: I don't want to disturb you. I just want to sit down and take a quiet drink.

(IRENE looks up at LOUIS then turns away.)

IRENE: I don't mind.

LOUIS: I can stand if you like but I'm tired out and I would quite like a seat.

(Pause.)

All right, then?

(IRENE says nothing, LOUIS sits down.) I'm sorry.

IRENE: What for?

LOUIS: Nudging your train of thought onto a different track. Derailing it. A little mix-up at the junctions. *(Pause.)*

I work on the railways.

But I don't speak like this all the time.

IRENE: I don't think anybody could. Too much of a strain.

LOUIS: True.

(Pause.)

But I thought you might like to know in case you're maybe thinking it's a little madness that's licking me down.

IRENE: No, I don't think you're mad.

LOUIS: No? I'm glad. For all I want to do in truth is to sit down and take a quiet drink and be on my way.

(IRENE looks sharply at him.)

Out into the cold and foggy London streets where the light spills carelessly from lamp to tramp.

IRENE: Where?

LOUIS: And from around the lazy corner the sharp leathery clicking of the dull man's shoes echoes in the chilly fifties air. Tonight, dark starry night, the dusky stranger plunges deeper and deeper into the moonlit abyss of hell.

IRENE: You sound like a loony even if you're not one.

LOUIS: Loony, lunatic, lunar, moon, moonlit. We're on the same wavelength.

IRENE: We are?

(Pause.)

LOUIS: They used to tell me I was a poet. At school.

IRENE: You work on the railways.

LOUIS: Things are hard at the moment.

(Pause.)

We go in a barber shop and they tell us they don't know how to cut a coloured man's hair rather than they don't want to cut a coloured man's hair. I can't even get a haircut. That's how bad things are. And getting worse.

IRENE: Things haven't been much different for some of us. One frigging crisis after another and all for what?

LOUIS: You know the saying, 'If things are bad for the populus then they are impossible for the poet'?

IRENE: I never did read much.

LOUIS: I just made it up.

IRENE: Well then how am I supposed to have heard it before?

LOUIS: I don't know. It's just a way of saying something.

(Pause.)

Sorry. I didn't want to disturb you.

IRENE: That's all right.

(Pause.)

You're not disturbing me.

(Pause.)

Am I disturbing you?

LOUIS: Even when the small child peers at the hummingbird from behind a low bush he still disturbs the bird for the bird knows.

(Pause.)

Tell the lone shark that he must come to a party up in the hills with the deer and the wild pig and the fowl, and play amongst the hibiscus with the monkey. Tell him so and see what happens. The shock of it will kill him. He can't last. Kill him dead, pow, dead like a piece of driftwood washed up on a lazy beach at sunset.

(Pause.)

Dead like a bird that flies too close to the sun. Pow!

(Pause.)

Dead like an Englishman on a summer's day. Dead.

(Pause.)

Dead.

IRENE: Dead?

LOUIS: Dead.

IRENE: You must have been drinking. Before you came in here.

LOUIS: Where?

IRENE: *Cross and Anchor* for instance.

LOUIS: *Cross and Anchor*?

IRENE: You know the *Cross and Anchor*. Further up the Grove. Paddy Sullivan's place. Big place. Used to be nice. When it first opened.

(Pause.)

You've heard of Paddy Sullivan. Drunk the Holyhead to Dublin ferry dry Christmas '53, '54 and '55, before they banned him. Rumour has it they paid him off if he wouldn't travel on it again, which is how he made it from navvy to landlord without so much as a bat of an eyelid.

Others say the IRA gave him some money for killing a man. Loyalist man it must have been.

(Pause.)

Bit fanciful that one, even for these parts.

(Pause.)

The old man, Jack, he was from Ireland, Dublin proper. Used to piss it up with Paddy Sullivan every night towards the end till I told him where to get off.

LOUIS: To get off?

IRENE: You know, piss off, on his bike. Take a long walk off a short pier.

LOUIS: I see now.

IRENE: He finally got the message. Eight years of rubbish.

(Pause.)

First year was the best year. Visiting Mum on a Sunday.

(Pause.)

LOUIS: There are too many coloured men in this country at one time. And the children we left behind with the women, they are going to end up more women than men. Just pretty-waisted men. Sexy prisoners to England, visiting Mum on a Sunday.

(He laughs, then stops. Pause.)

But maybe they're soon going to have to start sending us the food parcels and the clothes. We, the pioneers, to make life bearable for them. Slaves.

(IRENE reaches across and puts her hand on his.)

IRENE: You're shivering. Are you cold?

LOUIS: Have you ever felt a snowflake sting?

IRENE: Have you just come in here for a warm or do you want another drink?

LOUIS: No, no, no…

(Pause.)

I would like another drink please.

IRENE: Another pint then, Casey Jones.

LOUIS: Casey who?

IRENE: Another pint?

LOUIS: My name is not Casey.

IRENE: Sorry. *(She stands.)* Guinness?

(He looks at her and nods. She moves off. LOUIS begins to hum along nervously with the song on the jukebox and he looks anxiously around. He takes out a pack of ten cigarettes and taps them on the side of the table to the beat. IRENE comes back with a pint of Guinness and a bottle of light ale for herself. She sets them down on the table and sits.) Do you need a match because I haven't got one.

(LOUIS pushes the cigarettes back into his pocket.)

LOUIS: I can't afford it. I'm saving up for the future.

(Pause.)

IRENE: Do you like this music?

LOUIS: Why?

IRENE: I know you like music.

LOUIS: I suppose so. There's nothing wrong with a nice steady rhythm. A steady beat.

(Pause.)

A nice string band working up a mood or a pan ringing out in the still afternoon air when the school children begin to walk by the side of the road on their way home, their books on top of their heads to shield them from the sun. That's how I remember music.

(Pause.)

Stories keep breaking up inside me.

IRENE: What stories?

LOUIS: I'm sorry. I can't say everything I want to say. It's all messed up now.

IRENE: I was thinking of playing the jukebox if you'll lend us a tanner.

LOUIS: Sure, sure.

(He roots around in his pocket for one.)

IRENE: It's three for sixpence. You can have a choice too.

LOUIS: No, I trust you. You make the choice.

IRENE: If you're sure you trust me.

LOUIS: I'm going to have to trust you for I don't know the music too good.

IRENE: But do you trust me?

LOUIS: What?

(Pause. IRENE gets up and goes to the jukebox.)

IRENE: Do you want something special?

LOUIS: If you like.

IRENE: What?

LOUIS: Spiritual.

IRENE: Hymns?

LOUIS: I don't believe in God anymore. I'm not a child anymore.

IRENE: That's not right. You should have told me.

(She chooses the music and sits. It starts up again.)

But it's up to you, I suppose. I sometimes wonder myself.

LOUIS: There's nothing wrong with wondering. Unless you start to do too much of it.

(Pause.)

IRENE: Are you really a poet? I mean, have you ever really thought seriously about writing some of your stuff down?

(Pause.)

I can help, you know.

LOUIS: How?

IRENE: I can write letters, can't I? I can ring people up and tell them about you.

LOUIS: My mother said I had good hair and thin lips. In time I could be somebody. Back home. If I followed the true path of the Lord and righteousness. A poet even, but

243

you're right. I'm just talking foolishness. Poetry and that sort of thing is for rich white people. *(Pause.)*

Good hair and thin lips.

IRENE: You look all right to me as you are.

LOUIS: I cut cane to start with.

(Pause.)

My father said as long as the sun shines and the night falls, as long as the soil is rich and the rain hard and sharp, a man can cut cane. Now all that can happen and if a man can't think of a word of poetry to say he's going to stand and look down as his trousers ease their way over his shrinking waist, then his hips, then slither down his backside and leave the man high and dry and looking a damn fool.

(Pause.)

My father had some funny ways of putting things but he was always a truthful man, always told it like it was even when he knew it was going to hurt.

(Pause.)

Like when he told me, a ten-year-old boy, that coloured men shouldn't think too much.

(Pause.)

IRENE: Jack used to work in books, you know.

LOUIS: Books, newspapers, pamphlets, leaflets, I like them all. England is good for that. I can't beat her there.

(Pause.)

But it's not like what they said it would be. People are bad here. Bad, bad.

IRENE: Not everybody.

LOUIS: Everybody.

IRENE: That's not fair.

LOUIS: Yes everybody…

IRENE: But you can't…

LOUIS: What about the books?

(Pause.)

IRENE: I was going to tell you.

(Pause.)

The thing was, the only kind of books I ever saw him with had pictures of naked women in them. Used to leave the filth around the house for anyone to see. Got so as I couldn't even ask a friend around in case one was under a cushion or in the bog.

LOUIS: It's only that he used to read?

IRENE: He was a dealer in the stuff. Porn. Hard porn.

LOUIS: He was older than you?

IRENE: Still is. Eight years. Married him when I was nineteen. He was twenty-seven then but he had a decent job at least. Joiner for a firm building a range of flats down Wandsworth way. It was great then. Visiting Mum on a Sunday.

(Pause.)

After work he'd come home, have a bath, then we'd go out clubbing it or pubbing it. Somewhere different every night, loads to spend, and end up pissed by midnight then back home slowly, to avoid the coppers. He was great then, in the first year. But then the job finished and he started to get into some dodgy jobs and the money stopped and that's when the books started. I'm boring, aren't I?

(Pause.)

I kicked him out like I told you I did. He didn't leave me.

LOUIS: Kicked him out?

IRENE: Told him to leave, to go, to move on.

LOUIS: Which is what I did.

IRENE: No you didn't. I didn't ask you to...

LOUIS: Flee. Flee beauty like him.

IRENE: So you think I'm beautiful then, do you? Is that what you're trying to say?

LOUIS: You're like the island. You're a woman.

IRENE: What's that supposed to mean?

LOUIS: All islands are women. Except England. England is so hard she must be a man.

IRENE: Is it like in Africa over there? You know. The films.

(Pause.)

Humphrey Bogart. Katharine Hepburn. *The African Queen.*

(Pause.)

I just wondered.

LOUIS: I don't have anything to do with those people. I don't eat bananas on the top deck of a double-decker bus, and I don't walk around with my head in a damn book and tell all the girls my name is 'Prince' this, or 'Duke' the other.

IRENE: I know you don't.

LOUIS: Some of those African people make me sick.

(Pause.)

I'm a British subject.

IRENE: Object, isn't it? *(Pause.)*

LOUIS: I'm a British object.

IRENE: Watching the smoke curl aimlessly across a grey
skyline…

LOUIS: Watching the smoke curl aimlessly across a grey
skyline…

IRENE: Feeling the cold bitter air snapping into my sun-kissed
face…

LOUIS: Feeling the cold bitter air snapping into my sun-kissed
face…

IRENE: Dreaming of home.

LOUIS: Dreaming of home.

(Pause.)

IRENE: I like you Louis because you're not worn out even
though you keep saying you are.

(Pause.)

If things were different then they'd be different and
everything would be okay.

LOUIS: Maybe.

(Pause.)

There's more now. I thought of it today. Shunting.

IRENE: What?

LOUIS: Shunting. The Liverpool train into the depot. I was
shunting at the time when I thought of it.

IRENE: I'm glad. I thought it was a dirty word for a minute.
He went a bit that way when he started on the books.
Used to try words out on me.

(Pause.)

At first I used to blush and cry sometimes. Then I stopped
pretending I'd never heard them before and I started to
repeat them back to him. Made him so mad he started
to hit me then. Never a punch that might leave a mark,
always a slap, sting rather than bruise. Always room for
saying I'm sorry with a slap but not with a punch: a punch
is too definite.

(Pause.)

Jesus Christ, he used to make a sound when he got drunk
though. Like a dog when you keep standing on its tail all
the time. I couldn't stand him or his noises. I married a
man and ended up with a pig. Till I met you.

(Pause.)

I'd never seen a man cry till I met you.

LOUIS: Whilst I was shunting.

IRENE: I know. I haven't forgotten. Sorry.

(Pause.)

It's over a year now since I told him to go, isn't it? Fourteen
months to be exact. He'll be thirty-five in the springtime.
He called it April. I like calling it the springtime.

LOUIS: I know you do.

(Pause.)

My woman's smile is like a jagged knife.

IRENE: Is this it, then? The shunting poem. Can you shunt to it?

(She laughs.)

LOUIS: It cuts deep, bleeds ugly, drains life
From a man like me, born to be free
And live in the shadow of a hot, deep sea.

(Pause.)

IRENE: I don't get what you're trying to say.

LOUIS: My woman's touch is like a hunk of stone
It wounds and shivers and chills you to the bone
Her face, I loathe, her manners I hate,
And she thinks she can trap me with little grey bait.

(Pause.)

IRENE: I haven't done anything on purpose, Louis. It can still work out any way you want it to. *(Pause.)*

Don't expect me to beg.

LOUIS: High above the fields, and just a little below the clouds,
The wind whispers through the trees, ignoring the clouds,
Out yonder floats a spot, like a thin black slither,
This cruel boat taking people, my people, to where they will shiver; wither and die. *(Pause.)*

IRENE: All you have to say is that you don't regret anything. That's all I really want you to say.

LOUIS: Maybe I could turn it into a calypso and make some money that way, make my English fortune.

(As he begins to go through the last poem again, this time singing it to a calypso beat, IRENE tries to speak to him over the noise.)

IRENE: I didn't expect to see you in here. I was just lonely. I just wanted a quiet drink. *(He comes to the end of the poem and repeats the last line.)*

LOUIS: Shiver, wither and die.

(Pause.)

Shiver, wither and die. It doesn't seem to go in. More like a hymn ending.

IRENE: We can make it work but we just have to try harder than the others.

(Pause.)

You said that, didn't you?

LOUIS: Maybe one of the other ones will fit better to the calypso beat.

IRENE: But I don't want to hear any of them anymore.

LOUIS: So what happen? You don't like my poetry?

IRENE: People are starting to look at us.

LOUIS: People look at us anyway, Irene. Stare at us, for over a year now, like they're thinking they should be fucking, not out shopping for furniture, or at the pictures enjoying themselves, or on a bus going home, or having a drink, they think we should be fucking. *(He slaps the table.)*

They should be fucking.

(He slaps the table.)

They should be fucking.

(He slaps the table.)

They should be fucking.

IRENE: Louis, please, people are watching.

(LOUIS gets up and starts to fumble with his trousers.)

LOUIS: We should be fucking, you and I, West Indian man and English woman.

IRENE: For God's sake, Louis, sit down.

(She pushes him down into his seat.)

Don't behave like that. Don't let them get to you like that.

LOUIS: But don't you see how they look, hoping we won't do anything human like laugh, or cry, or kiss.

IRENE: Please.

LOUIS: Kiss me.

(She moves to do so.)

I don't mean on the cheek either. I mean properly. Like you mean it in truth.

IRENE: I do.

LOUIS: Well, if you mean it just kiss me full and let them watch.

(IRENE leans forward and they kiss. They hold for a moment, then break.)

IRENE: I don't care about them.

LOUIS: Are they still watching?

IRENE: Yes.

(Pause.)

We'll never be able to come in here for a drink again but I don't mind.

LOUIS: A drink?

IRENE: I said I didn't mind. I don't.

LOUIS: A man can go anywhere in this country for a drink, so they tell us. It's a free country so come and take a drink where you like, brother, so long as you don't fall in love with any of our women. Fuck them, in private, by all means, but don't make them feel happy. Just make them feel grateful then leave them and take a drink where you like.

IRENE: Why are you going on like this?

LOUIS: So, we can drink someplace else.

IRENE: I know.

LOUIS: Do you want to continue to care in public?

IRENE: I don't know what you are talking about, Louis. All I know is I felt safe in here. I felt safe in here with you too.

LOUIS: Safe?

IRENE: Safe. But you don't care about me anymore so why pretend you do? After a year you just disappear into the middle of the night.

(Pause.)

Doesn't it matter to you how I feel?

LOUIS: A man once warned me that when I get to England not to get involved with any of the white women for you can't take them back home with you for as soon as they set foot on the island they're going to start crying out for

a handmaiden and a butler and a maid, and how the hell
can a cane-cutter afford such things?

IRENE: Don't talk stupid, Louis.

LOUIS: And the man who told me this went on and told me
that women are just like a bowl of exotic fruit, and he
likes to take a bite from them all, taste them a little, but he
doesn't like to linger too long for when you get through to
the core they are just like all fruit: hard, stony and bitter.

IRENE: I don't want to know those things...

LOUIS: And the man who told me this was my wife's father.

(Pause.)

Pushed his finger up into my face the night before I left
and warned me that when I get to England not to get
involved with any of the white women for you can't take
them back home with you.

IRENE: He was just trying to put you off.

LOUIS: He didn't have to. I'd already made up my mind I
wanted nothing to do with you.

IRENE: But you didn't know me.

LOUIS: White women.

(Pause.)

I was going to work, save, and send for my wife when the
time came, when I could feel proud enough to support her in
a better style of life than she was accustomed to back home.

IRENE: But you said she went off with a fisherman.

LOUIS: She probably felt safe with him.

(Pause.)

First time I ever saw a white woman in England I knew I wanted one. Not necessarily to keep but so I could keep it if I wanted to.

IRENE: You told me this.

LOUIS: I'm not talking about you, though. I'm talking about before I met you. When I first came here.

IRENE: I don't know what to think anymore.

LOUIS: But it's how it was. I wanted one. Like a child wants the latest toy. But it's not the child's life it ruins but the father's pocket. *(Pause.)*

The father can always get a new pair of pants.

(Pause. The music stops. IRENE reaches across and takes his hand.)

IRENE: You look frightened, Louis.

LOUIS: I don't look like nothing. Frightened is too definite. I look like nothing.

IRENE: The music has stopped.

LOUIS: If you want an all-year-round suntan for your children then marry to a coloured man. You can always call the child medium-rare.

(Pause. IRENE stares at him. Then she stands. He reaches down into his pockets and pushes sixpence across the table to her. She touches his hand as she takes up the money. He notices but says nothing. She puts the money in the jukebox.)

IRENE: There's not much we haven't played.

(She begins to punch out her choices. Then she starts to sing to the song.)

LOUIS: Over two years in this place now and I still feel like a sparrow not an eagle.

(IRENE comes back and sits down.)

IRENE: No, Louis.

LOUIS: These people, they break you by smiling at you one
day and ignoring you the next, by their hateful toleration,
by crossing the damn road when they see the two of us
coming.

(Pause.)

You people are such good dancers
We bet you're good in bed
We bet you're also good runners
But you don't have much in your heads.

IRENE: They don't say that anymore, though.

LOUIS: It's older than the national anthem.

(Pause.)

It is the national anthem.

(Pause.)

In those first few weeks I used to go for long walks past
buildings that looked like they were closed. Everywhere
looked like it was closed. Then I'd come a little closer and
find they were really open, that there was light, and I used
to go inside and find these dead people playing games on
green tables, or drinking, or listening to greasy music, and
asking me questions like, 'Is your father a king?', and 'Do
you prefer eating white people or coloured people?', and
in one of these open-closed places I met a man so lonely
that everywhere he went he carried his suitcase with him
just to remind him that one day he's soon going to be
leaving this place.

(Pause.)

And then out again into the street where the lights are so bright that sometimes it looks clearer at night than in the day. And then it would start up again. The rain. The rain, slanting hail tearing at exposed flesh. When you can't afford a jacket or an overcoat even. And I stop and think by the side of the road.

(Pause.)

Do you know how long it is since I've seen the sea?

(Pause.)

IRENE: Haven't you ever liked it here?

LOUIS: I lost my nerve. I don't fly close to the sun no more.

(Pause.)

The lights of the Empire Cinema in Leicester Square. You can't believe what that means to a grown man from a small island where only six or seven houses have proper electricity. Two years ago Louis White stands outside a cinema and cries. A cinema, girl, not a Buckingham Palace or Houses of Parliament. A cinema. And the traffic lights, roundabouts, lampposts, chimney pots like skyscrapers to me, and people pouring down the streets at the end of the day like it's World War Two about to break out again. And me hiding in shop doorways scared out of my mind, girl. Taking shelter in a shop doorway in Oxford Street.

(Pause.)

I'm writing such rich letters back home. Even British Railways smelt sweet that first year and when she left me for the fisherman I just wrote and told her good luck. No hard feelings, no regrets. I'm upset, for the girl was something to me, but no regrets. I'm in England. The earth is a platform, not an anchor, to a man like me.

IRENE: I remember you saying that.

LOUIS: You don't remember for when I made it up I had never met you as yet.

IRENE: I remember you telling me, though. When we first met in that awful club.

LOUIS: *The Z Club.*

IRENE: I could see it was starting to get to you then.

LOUIS: No. Nothing bothered me in those days.

IRENE: It did, Louis. You know it did.

LOUIS: You think I'm different from a white man?

(Pause.)

Better and less in one?

IRENE: Of course you're different. You're different from any man.

LOUIS: I think I know why they look at us.

IRENE: It doesn't matter.

LOUIS: So they can cry 'progress' and vomit at the same time.

(Pause.)

IRENE: Don't let it get to you. Not now.

LOUIS: I want to go.

IRENE: Where?

LOUIS: I don't know.

IRENE: Finish your drink first.

(Pause.)

LOUIS: If you feel safe with me why do you always look so fearful when coloured people, especially coloured women, look at you?

(Pause.)

I notice how you look, you know. Your eyes dropping slightly, your face making an aimless smile, your grip tightening in my hand, or on my leg.

IRENE: I'm not afraid.

(Pause.)

LOUIS: I feel the same way sometimes. Hurts, makes you feel foolish for a minute.

(Pause.)

I look around and wonder how many road accidents we're going to cause today.

(Pause.)

It's us who these white people are going to riot about.

IRENE: Why?

LOUIS: Nigger and nigger-lover. They don't really hate the coloured man with a brick in one hand and terror in his eyes for they're used to that from slavery days. What they are not used to is a coloured man with a white woman on one arm and a spring in his step. *(Pause.)*

We've done it, Irene.

IRENE: Done what?

LOUIS: Turned over our hostages to fortune…in England.

(He laughs.)

Look at them. These people here who make you feel safe. You know what they think of you? Pervert. Easy screw. Whore. Black man's white woman. She must have three breasts or bad breath or she fucked the West Indian cricket team on their last tour or her father must have fucked her when she was a child and that made her go funny.

(Pause. He laughs.)

Whore. Whore. Whore.

IRENE: I know what they say! I know what they think!

LOUIS: And you can live with it? You're happy to live like that?

IRENE: I can only live with it if you can. I can't do it if you keep saying all this, nobody can.

LOUIS: I want to go home.

IRENE: Then let's go home.

LOUIS: No. I mean home, home. Back home.

IRENE: I see.

(Pause.)

LOUIS: Depression is eating me out, Irene.

IRENE: I know.

(Pause.)

LOUIS: I want to go home alone.

IRENE: I'll give you what money I have if it'll help.

LOUIS: No. You'll need it.

IRENE: Come home with me tonight but don't just go in the middle of the night again. Wait till morning then you can go. I won't try to stop you. *(Pause.)*

LOUIS: I have to go for I just don't like what is happening to me here.

(Pause.)

IRENE: Do you hate me?

LOUIS: I don't hate.

(Pause.)

Are you with them?

IRENE: With who?

LOUIS: Them.

(He points at the other people in the pub. Pause.)

Or are you with me?

IRENE: I want to be with you.

LOUIS: For the baby's sake?

IRENE: I had to tell you last night. I mean, you had to know sometime, didn't you? Didn't you?

(Pause.)

You're more important to me than the baby.

LOUIS: I don't want you.

(Pause.)

I can't afford the butler.

(Pause.)

I don't mean it.

(Pause.)

I don't know if you talk to them about me. I don't know if you see the teeth behind their smile. I should never have touched you. I should never have come to play amongst the hibiscus.

(IRENE reaches over to touch him.) Don't touch me, Irene.

(Pause. IRENE stands up.)

IRENE: I'm going now, if that's what you want.

(LOUIS looks away.)

I said I'm going now.

(Pause.) Louis?

(Pause.)

Louis, if you don't want the baby I can always get rid of it.

(He looks up at her.) But I won't.

(Pause.)

You don't have to see me again.

(Pause.)

I'm used to being on my own.

(She begins to cry.)

I'm not much use to you anymore, am I?

LOUIS: Use?

IRENE: But at least I can still fight. The right things.

(Pause.)

I won't forget you.

LOUIS: You're not going to forget me?

IRENE: I'm not…no, it doesn't matter.

LOUIS: Of course it matters. Everything matters in this country. Dirty milk bottles matter. Raggedy pants on a washing line matter.

(IRENE bends forward and kisses LOUIS on the cheek.)

IRENE: Goodbye, Louis.

LOUIS: They're still watching.

IRENE: I know they are but it doesn't matter. It really doesn't matter.

(His eyes follow her across the floor and out of the pub. The jukebox heaves itself to life again and he takes a drink and looks nervously around.)

(Lights fade.)

END OF PLAY